The entrepreneurial journey can be a lon[...] with people who are going through the d[...] enterprise can almost be likened to discovering an oasis in the desert every week. Joel Freeman has put together an **exceptional book and companion workbook for entrepreneurs**, which can be used for **personal development or to connect business owners in your church** on a regular basis. It's my hunch that every participating entrepreneur will become more successful and smarter as a result. I hope that large and small churches alike also understand the **ministry potential** of Freeman's innovative idea for the Entrepreneur Ministry Club Connections (emc²). It's an **excellent "easy-to-implement, follow-the-bouncing-ball" idea** that every church might want to consider.

> — DR. TONY EVANS
> Senior Pastor, Oak Cliff Bible Church, President, Urban Alternatives

Most pastors don't consider themselves "entrepreneurs," but the word simply means "a person who organizes, manages, and assumes the risks of an enterprise." If that doesn't describe what Christian workers do, what does? In Joel Freeman's book-workbook combination **you will find valuable information and motivation** to help make you the best possible servant-leader and will also provide the necessary resources for entrepreneurs in your church to **start an entrepreneur ministry club connection** (emc²). Let's learn from the business world as we carry on the Lord's business!

> — WARREN W. WIERSBE
> Author, former pastor of Moody Church

God has given me the honor to have known and worked with Joel Freeman for a number of years. His newest book, titled *If Nobody Loves You, Create the Demand,* examines the joys and heartaches of the entrepreneurial journey. He has also developed a **practical, group-friendly workbook**, connecting the contents of the book specifically to entrepreneurs who live out their faith in the marketplace every day. Joel's entrepreneurial book-workbook combination is an **excellent catalyst to assist with developing and empowering small-business owners** and those interested in impacting their communities in a meaningful way.

> — JOHN JENKINS
> Senior Pastor, First Baptist Church of Glenarden

I have at least fifty books people have given me to read, and I really felt nothing would probably come out of reading Joel Freeman's new book. But the title intrigued me. As I began glancing over the book, the book really began to speak to me and my current situation, and it became a real 'God moment' for me. As I continued to read, I was **pleasantly surprised**. Finally a book that really gave me something besides trying to get me to attend another conference or buy the author's next book! Much of the information in Dr. Freeman's book was new and extremely insightful. The book has helped fill my speaking calendar and has given me a major strategy going into the future. This is an **extremely helpful book** for anyone trying to better market what they do. Anyone, young or old, will greatly benefit from reading this book. I am especially interested in the Entrepreneur Ministry Club Connection (**emc²**). It is my opinion that **every church can benefit by using this book and workbook**—developing a regular meeting especially designed for entrepreneurs in their churches. It will be an experience that will bring practical entrepreneurial wisdom to all of the participants and also will allow everyone to better apply spiritual principles to their business enterprises.

— KEN JOHNSON

Chaplain, NFL Super Bowl Champion, Indianapolis Colts, 2007

If you're a dreamer, *If Nobody Loves You, Create the Demand* is for you. Dr. Freeman has **harnessed the wisdom of the ages** and added his own solid teaching to it. If you're a doer, the accompanying workbook connects the contents of that book to entrepreneurs. Joel Freeman's resources are **essential reading on your way to the top**.

— SOLOMON HICKS

Author, entrepreneur, business coach, and motivational speaker

if nobody loves you

CREATE
THE DEMAND

WORKBOOK

if nobody loves you

CREATE

THE DEMAND

WORKBOOK

A Powerful Jolt of
Entrepreneurial
Energy and Wisdom

JOEL A. FREEMAN

Authentic

COLORADO SPRINGS · MILTON KEYNES · HYDERABAD

Authentic Publishing
We welcome your questions and comments.

USA   1820 Jet Stream Drive, Colorado Springs, CO 80921 www.authenticbooks.com
UK   9 Holdom Avenue, Bletchley, Milton Keynes, Bucks, MK1 1QR
       www.authenticmedia.co.uk
India Logos Bhavan, Medchal Road, Jeedimetla Village, Secunderabad 500 055, A.P.

If Nobody Loves You, Create the Demand Workbook
ISBN-13: 978-1-606570-20-3

Copyright © 2009 by Joel A. Freeman, Ph.D

12 11 10 09 / 6 5 4 3 2 1

It was Gary S. Paxton's song title "If Nobody Loves You, Create the Demand" that inspired the
title of the book that, in turn, inspired this workbook. Thank you, Gary.

A percentage of the profits of this book will go to The Freeman Institute® Foundation.
FreemanInstituteFoundation.org

All Scripture quotations, unless otherwise indicated, are taken from the *Holy Bible, New
International Version®. NIV®*. Copyright © 1973, 1978, 1984 by International Bible Society.
Used by permission of Zondervan. All rights reserved.

Scripture quotations marked NKJV are taken from the New King James Version. Copyright ©
1982 by Thomas Nelson, Inc. Used by permission. All rights reserved.

Scripture quotations marked NLT are taken from the *Holy Bible*, New Living Translation,
copyright © 1996, 2004. Used by permission of Tyndale House Publishers, Inc., Wheaton,
Illinois 60189. All rights reserved.

Scripture quotations marked KJV are takend from the *Authorized King James Version*. Public
domain.

Cover and interior design: projectluz.com
Editorial team: Kay Larson, Erika Bremer

Printed in the United States of America

CONTENTS

emc^2
Entrepreneur Ministry Club Connection

EVERYTHING RELATIVE TO YOU,
YOUR BUSINESS, AND YOUR PURPOSE IN LIFE

Entrepreneur clubs provide excellent opportunities for individual or group mentoring—a great place for "solutionists," ready to provide practical advice and realistic solutions for the myriad of issues that most entrepreneurs face. The book-workbook combination is especially designed for the following individuals who are trying to live out their faith in practical ways in their respective enterprises:

- **Pre-Entrepreneur**: Someone who is thinking about taking the leap into his or her own business—"kicking the tires" to see if this is something that might be a viable option for the future.

- **Budding Entrepreneur**: Someone who has already taken the leap and is into the first phases of entrepreneurship. Many are evening or weekend entrepreneurs. Things are exciting, going well, confusing, stressful, failing, or too much to handle (in a good way).

- **Seasoned/Serial Entrepreneur**: Someone who has a fair amount of experience, looking for ways to share his or her expertise with others. There are also opportunities to learn new things and to get a recharge in personal passion for business—especially if one is experiencing mild forms of jadedness and complacency.

- **Corporate Entrepreneur**: Someone who works in a corporate environment that requires a fair amount of entrepreneurship (e.g., radio-ad sales, automobile sales, research, pastoring, engineering, etc.).

- **Turnkey Entrepreneur**: Someone involved in an organization (e.g., direct sales, network marking, franchise, real estate, etc.) that has spent millions of dollars in research, developing a certain protocol that can work well for anyone who has the passion to succeed—a safety net, a system that can be duplicated for most anyone in any region of the country/world. Entrepreneurship within the system is something that each individual can determine as time goes by.

Social entrepreneurship is the umbrella under which the aforementioned individuals choose to operate. A **social entrepreneur** wants to be socially responsible, with business enterprises that allow them to "do good while doing well."

Why Does Every Church Need to Establish Something Like an Entrepreneur Ministry Club Connection (emc²)?

As with *If Nobody Loves You, Create the Demand*, I have developed a workbook version that will get right to the point and will give you plenty of things to think about and discuss with others. You may also choose to utilize the book-workbook combination solely as a vehicle for personal development.

The greater purpose of the workbook is to expose you to the collective wisdom of others on a regular basis. My objective for developing this additional resource is to offer your emc² group the "give-and-take" framework for discussing real-world business issues within a Spirit-filled, biblical context.

Developing and enhancing a small business introduces one to the ups and the downs of life. The entrepreneurial journey challenges an individual and/or family members on a number of levels to:

- Discern the difference between a viable business dream and a nightmare.

- Know what questions to ask when researching business models and legal issues.

- Explore personal doubts, hopes, goals, self-talk, and fears.

- Affirm the part that prayer plays in business success.

- Embrace the purpose of business.

- Discuss investment, saving, insurance, and tithing issues.

- Learn how to respond to valid and/or "uncalled-for" criticism from family and friends.

- Examine personal work ethics. Challenging the extremes, like workaholism and laziness.

- Keep afloat—financially, mentally, emotionally, physically, and spiritually.

- Learn how to work both hard and smart.

- Deal with long hours, stress, and family relationships—especially during the first few ramp-up years of any business venture.

- Answer the question: Can husbands and wives work together in the same business? If so, how?

- Develop an ongoing care of business partnerships.

- Understand how the good is the enemy of the best.

- Learn how not to get sidetracked by distractions.

- Apply the principles of diversification and multiplication without losing momentum in the core business focus.

- Take time to count the many blessings—gratitude for the God-given skills, abilities, and relationships necessary for the development of a successful business.

- Develop group and personal definitions of success that are motivated by values that will still be important a thousand years from now.

- Understand gentle accountability.

- Apply eternal truths to time-measured goals and objectives.

- Increase the potential of doing good while doing well.

What better place than the church to address these issues and more?

> Do not let this Book of the Law depart from your mouth; meditate on it day and night, so that you may be careful to do everything written in it. Then you will be prosperous and successful.—Joshua 1:8

Wise business sense connected with the Word of God, the presence of the Holy Spirit, and seasoned entrepreneurs is a winning combination. It is my hope and my prayer that everyone who becomes a committed member of a Bible-centered, Spirit-filled emc² group will become wildly prosperous and successful—for an eternal purpose.

Benefits of an emc² Entrepreneur Ministry Club Connection in your church:

To connect with and learn from various people representing stages of the entrepreneurial journey who are committed to speaking the truth about faith, works, grace, relationships, and eternal value in a confidential atmosphere of respectful encouragement in regularly scheduled meetings.

Commit to reading the designated chapter of the *If Nobody Loves You . . .* book and also the information in this workbook. Write your responses to the workbook questions in a separate notebook (provided by you) so that you will be ready to discuss each of the questions for the next meeting.

INREACH:

1. The domino effect: As small-business owners succeed, they will have more resources available to help in their community and/or church.
2. Community building: Sometimes church-related relationships are one-dimensional and shallow: "Hi, how are you? Fine. Good to see you again. See you next week. God bless you." An entrepreneur club allows the participants to see unique qualities in each other and to know of the various businesses represented in the church. Like anything else in life, shared experiences permit one to speak with greater authority to others who may be experiencing something similar (e.g., death of a loved one, drug/alcohol addiction, child rearing, wedding planning, etc.). Small-business owners and entrepreneurs have that same kind of a fraternity of shared experiences.

OUTREACH:

1. Reality-based relationships: Men and women who are not inclined to attend a regular church service may be more open to attending an entrepreneur club that is designed to scratch real-world itches.
2. Networking: Local/regional entrepreneurs who have experienced success and are willing to share their stories can be invited to join the group.

We have minted beautiful bronze coins that each member can keep as a reminder of their commitment to the emc^2 group and also as an inspirational reminder. The front of each coin states, "if nobody loves you" while the rear states, "CREATE The Demand."—a reminder that if nothing is happening, it's up to you to take the steps required to make something happen. Your leader will know how to get them in quantity . . . one for each emc^2 member. More information is available at www.emc2clubs.com.

Facilitator/Leader's Guidelines Online:
information, blog, comments, and suggestions for facilitators at
emc2Leaders.com

It is our hope that this website will become a living, breathing community of facilitators who share what is working and what is not working in their respective clubs. You can help make it happen.

The Entrepreneur Connection is a FREE radio program (seventy-two five-minute programs) built around the audio version of the book, designed to educate and inspire listeners about the entrepreneurial journey. You might know of a local college radio station, a non-commercial FM radio station, or an Internet-based station that might be interested. Contact them about this entrepreneur radio program. If they qualify, we'd be happy to send them a free CD with all of the radio programs (mp3 format) ready to be played once a week for seventy-two weeks. The station GM might even place a tag at the end of each program letting listeners know about your entrepreneur club. Check out the website for more detailed information.

eConnectRadio.com

How would your emc² group like to develop a relevant outreach tool for your church, along with an opportunity for other business owners in your congregation and community to advertise their respective goods and services? See the ad about *everyday matters*® magazine in the back of this workbook.

YourLocalMag.com

AN ENTREPRENEURIAL JOURNEY
SHOE SHINE SECRETS

Start by doing what's necessary; then do what's possible;
and suddenly you are doing the impossible.
—St. Francis of Assisi

Each of us has a story about his or her personal entrepreneurial journey. Here's mine: I was infected by the entrepreneurial bug early on. I am not sure where it came from because neither of my parents possesses a fiber or cell of entrepreneurial inclination in their bodies. If the entrepreneurial bug had bitten them, they would have smacked it with a fly swatter.

When I was six years old (1960), my parents, Arthur and Katherine, with my brother, Steve, and sister, Nancy (Beth wasn't born yet), moved to Three Hills in Alberta, Canada. It was a small town of about two thousand, with nine ice hockey rinks. My dad ultimately took the position of the high school principal at Prairie Bible Institute (PBI). He led a team of teachers who trained the children of staff members, adult Bible school students, and other parents concerned about Christian training. Some students were from the local area, and others were dormitory students from around the world.

PBI was a unique school/community that began in the 1930s under the leadership of L. E. Maxwell, a man of immense vision, perseverance, and integrity. Anyone attending the school knew he or she would be coming to a spiritual boot camp. No parties. No prolonged fraternization with the opposite sex. No distractions. The school was designed to educate people in theology, global missions, and serious Bible study. Students such as Elisabeth Elliot, Don Richardson, and many others came from around the world. There were a lot of rules and regulations at that time; many were (in my opinion) legalistic.

The theme of the school at the time was Training Disciplined Soldiers for Christ. The Spartan buildings and remote location on the flat, treeless prairies, 160 miles from the Rocky Mountains, visually supported that motto. Every spring and fall there was a missions conference, attracting renowned speakers such as Alan Redpath, Major Ian Thomas, Don Richardson, and many others. It was an intriguingly wonderful place to grow up, with students from all over the world—Fiji, Congo, the United States, Thailand, Finland, and other places—walking the sidewalks. A "salad bowl" of international cultural diversity smack dab in the middle of the Canadian prairies.

Even though we never missed a meal, our family was quite poor, but we didn't know it. My parents never discussed our financial situation in a negative light—what some might call "poor-mouthing." My parents were grateful for everything.

The work ethic was a regular part of our lives as children. Washing dishes, shoveling snow in the winter, weeding the garden in the summer, cleaning our rooms year round, besides washing floors and many other duties, were required of each child. We all pulled our own weight. Grumbling and complaining were allowed in small doses but would never change the house rules.

The idea for my first business endeavor came to me one Sunday morning when I happened to notice a Bible school student's scruffy shoes as he walked by our pew. His shoes were crying out for a good polishing. No SWOT analysis was required before moving forward. That single glance was the only market research I needed. I was about ten years old.

Here's what my Saturdays looked like from that point on: After my chores were completed at home, I would make my way over to the Bible school men's dormitory to shine shoes. I knocked on every dorm room door every week. Ten cents for a pair of shoes and twenty-five cents for a pair of boots. Believe me, the guys who worked at the school farm got a great deal!

I began carrying a kitchen knife in my shoe shine kit for the special hard-to-scrape-cow-dung boot projects.

After several hours of hard work, I would exit the dormitory area, waddling across a field to my home, with every pocket bulging with coins.

I would then throw all of the coins on my bed, counting them several times, stacking the pennies, nickels, dimes, and quarters in separate columns on the floor, followed up by a recount—the closest I have ever gotten to King Midas and his obsessive need to count his riches.

Fast-forward to an image of me about seven years later—on the side of the road with my thumb out, looking for a ride. I was seventeen years of age, with a Texas-size chip on my shoulder. A rebel without a "pause." I hated my parents and everything they stood for. I left home with twenty-four dollars in my pocket. Bob Kirk, a close friend, and I set out hitchhiking to Vancouver and beyond. We were separated in Portland, Oregon. I continued south, living for months with relatives in Lodi, California. Some of this part of the story is told in my book *When Life Isn't Fair: Making Sense Out of Suffering*.

I traveled across country to Maine in 1972 and worked in a restaurant on the waterfront in Portland. I stayed with my sister, Nancy, and my brother-in-law, Bruce. He was a baker at a prestigious restaurant, and I was his helper. Baker's hours, four o'clock in the morning to eleven o'clock, five days a week, didn't permit me to have much of a nightlife.

I had a conversion experience on September 10, 1972, in a small church in Bath, Maine, and signed up for Bible school, which started the very next day. I worked full time as a construction worker, going to evening classes. It was an incredible time of spiritual and emotional growth for me.

About a year later, I called my parents, asking for forgiveness for the pain I had caused them. We all wept, and the Lord brought reconciliation to our family. Even though we were three thousand miles apart (Maine to Alberta), it was as though we were in the same room whenever we talked on the phone. I was ordained as a pastor in 1972.

During the eighteen years of pastoring (1975–1993), I brought my entrepreneurial instincts with me. Some pastors or businesspeople like to build upon what another has started. Other people like to start things. Starting churches from scratch has always been my modus operandi. I pioneered three churches (Friendship, Maine; Baltimore and Columbia, Maryland). The churches I started also sent out mission teams to Mayaguez, Puerto Rico, and Santo Domingo, Dominican Republic.

For nineteen wonderful years (1979–1998) I was also the chaplain for the NBA Washington Bullets/Wizards. As one of the first mentor/chaplains in the history of the NBA, this was also a classic entrepreneurial pursuit—charting new territory.

One year our church put on a charity auction with the famous boxer Sugar Ray Leonard as our honorary chairman. We had all sorts of signed sports memorabilia, antiques, household goods, services, and even an automobile. We raised almost twenty thousand dollars for a special project. It was a blast!

In 1978 I came up with the idea for *The Shepherd's Guide*®, a Christian business directory, with franchises in major cities all over North America. When I travel, I see copies of the guide in various cities and feel like a proud grandpa. I had the idea, , but ideas are a dime a dozen. It took someone such as Doug Scheidt to bring the concept to reality and to build upon it.

The entrepreneurial passion has always been a part of my life, regardless of what I was pursuing. I don't know where you began your entrepreneurial journey, but perhaps you can relate a bit to my story. I hope so.

The definition of an entrepreneur doesn't always include making a lot of money. The entrepreneurial spirit can motivate one person to join the Peace Corps or to become a missionary, working in a developing nation by helping farmers increase their coffee, rice, or banana crops. The same spirit may motivate another person to do pioneer work in the field of cancer or AIDS research. Still another person might become extremely successful selling automobiles so that he or she can financially help those who manifest their entrepreneurial spirit in other ways—locally, regionally, or globally. Regardless of your vocation or calling, it is all about being a blessing and leaving a legacy of blessing that increases God's fame around the world.

In Ralph Winter's book *The Kingdom Strikes Back*, his description of blessings is one of the best I have seen. He distinguishes between the common Western idea of *blessings* (plural) as material or social benefits, and the Hebrew ideas of *blessing* (singular) as relational realities which confer responsibility and obligation as well as privileges. Blessing is a distinctively familial idea. By extending His blessing throughout the ages, God is establishing an enormous family, an array of households of faith which together display His kingdom and His glory. I believe this is the blessing God's people are to become, which will be passed organically on to the next generation.

The workbook you now hold in your hands (along with the *If Nobody*

Loves You . . . book) is designed to give your group of entrepreneurs a pathway for establishing a regular encounter around the issues that you deal with on a daily basis. Your group will select the best cadence for such meetings.

You will need to purchase a notebook for completing assignments, writing your reflections, responding to questions, and expressing personal opinions about the many issues you will encounter. The notebook may also serve as a journal of your thoughts, feelings, and business decisions that can help you when writing your autobiography later in life.

Like the book version, I have developed a workbook that will not waste your time—giving you and your emc^2 group the framework for discussing real-world business issues within a biblical context and formulating life-long friendships. If you have already read my book you know that I am not a fan of get rich quick schemes. In my opinion, writers and speakers who export that kind of philosophy are committing "entrepreneurial malpractice." If they have had any business success at all, they know better. They know how long and how difficult the entrepreneurial journey can be sometimes.

IMPORTANT: It's all about doing good while doing well. I hope that the entrepreneur ministry club connections will help you establish deep, lifelong friendships. I also hope that the meetings will assist in your financial success so that you can not only provide well for your family, but also have more resources to help others in your church or community. Fulfill the assignment(s) God has given you with dignity and honor. My hope is that you have started well. Finish well.

Entrepreneurs generally do not fear failure. They fear not trying. Implementing a business dream is much more fun than trying to launch a business nightmare. Hopefully the group you connect with will help its members avoid the business nightmare scenarios. Even with great clients, a top-notch business plan, excellent support, a full bank account and good help, growing a business is tough—every day—and filled with ups and downs.

By the way, what's your story? Take some time to reflect upon your entrepreneurial journey, and then feel free to share it with the group at the first meeting you attend.

NGEclubs.com — Next Generation Entrepreneur Clubs (NGEC): A resource that connects the contents of this book to the lives of young adults (approximately fifteen to twenty-six years old). The website is developed especially for NGEC leaders, with ideas for establishing an NGEC in your school or community. The workbook-book-audio book combination can be an effective tool for helping to develop purpose for our next generation through the entrepreneurial gateway. Making plans for the future positively impacts present decisions and priorities.

How Your Personality Impacts Your Entrepreneurial Success

Before attending the first meeting, it is important for everyone to visit the website MyGreatPersonality.com. Why? Because the first meeting will focus upon the strengths and vulnerabilities of your personality. I would strongly suggest taking the Personality Style "photo album" version (with comprehensive overview of the way God designed you) and also the *Entrepreneur Attitude Assessment*. A small investment in your life that will reap rich dividends for a lifetime.

YOUR GREAT PERSONALITY

Ancient Wisdom

Proverbs 1:7: "The fear of the LORD is the beginning of knowledge, but fools despise wisdom."

Proverbs 8:17–18: "I love those who love me, and those who seek me find me. With me are riches and honor, enduring wealth and prosperity."

Proverbs 12:11: "He who works his land will have abundant food, but he who chases fantasies lacks judgment."

Reflections

As you think about the strengths and vulnerabilities of your personality style, what are your initial thoughts and feelings (positive and/or negative)?

What comments have friends, co-workers, clients, or relatives made about your personality over the years? Make a list of the compliments and/or criticisms and see if any positive or negative themes emerge that you can celebrate or improve.

What are some thoughts (if any) you have about how your personality impacts your business success?

Additional Perspectives

I heard once that 15 percent of financial and career success can be attributed to technical competence, while 85 percent is due to good interpersonal skills. I believe it. If this is true, understanding the way we are wired behaviorally is of paramount importance.

God designed all of us with different interests, skills, emotional pain thresholds, backgrounds, education, experiences, likes, dislikes, and much more. What impacts our personality the most: nurture (role models) or nature (genetics)? How about our unique physical characteristics?

The cruelest creatures on the planet are children. Let's go back to when we were kids. If you were too tall or too short, too skinny or too fat, certain kids in your neighborhood had special internal radar that could focus in on your Achilles' heel. They were unmerciful. Am I right? And if you moved to another city, the kids in that neighborhood had the same radar information.

What about your birth order? Were you a firstborn? You probably have always been comfortable around adults, and you always looked for the people in power to get things accomplished. Last born? Your parents were tuckered out by the time you came along. Only child? Your parents said, "We're never doing that again!" (Just kidding.) If you are in the middle somewhere, you may have struggled with your identity and significance. There are other categories, but you get the picture.

In addition to all that has been stated thus far, it has been said that emotionally painful experiences are the greatest modifier of human behavior. If you have been through a divorce, or if you have had a former business partner get "selective amnesia" after your joint business venture started making money, you know what I am talking about.

Emotional pain can change a person from a wide-eyed, your-word-and-a-handshake-is-enough visionary to a calculated, I-will-never-do-business-with-anyone-without-my-lawyer-and-a-contract cynic.

We are all fragile creatures—one hairbreadth away from insanity (not in a clinical sense), yet we also can tend to be quite stubborn. One thing for sure, you and I are unique individuals, with an assignment to use what we have been given for the honor and glory of our Creator.

God programs diversity into the church and then commands us to love each other. Is this an indication of his sense of humor? One could

Relationships: The Litmus Test of our Christianity

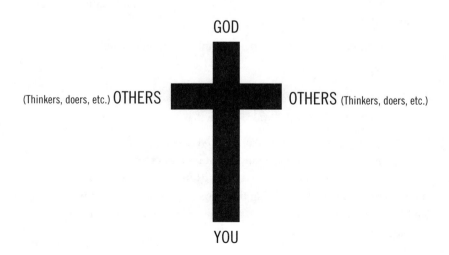

make that inference. There are vertical and horizontal components to our relationships.

There really is no cosmic conspiracy out there. We get on each other's nerves just by being ourselves.

Entrepreneurs generally do not work well with others on a team. Why? Because to start a small business requires the efforts of one person—YOU! The day-to-day operations are many—ranging from balancing the checkbook and making many phone calls to running business-related errands, shopping for office supplies, and marketing. If you don't do it, it doesn't get done.

As your business builds, you will have to hire people, or you'll have to bring on independent contractors to help with the expansion. Dealing with other people's issues can present inconvenient intrusions into the lifestyle of someone who has done everything up to that point. Delegating and letting go will become new personal growth opportunities. The development of a succession plan can become an even greater challenge.

Personality conflicts are generally near or at the top of the list when organizations try to figure out the main reasons for poor morale, diminished job performance, lack of teamwork, low productivity, or loss of creativity. And don't hold on to the erroneous view that Christian organizations are somehow exempt from conflict. It just ain't true.

The closer we get to the administrative center of any religious institution, business enterprise, family system, or neighborhood association, the more opportunities we have for disillusionment. Blessed disillusionment.

All of us have a particular dynamic, compelling force within. Whatever drives you—

- Getting things done. Task accomplishment in a punctual manner,

- Approval of others,

- Maintaining a manageable, easygoing pace,

- Attention to details. Making sure that everything is accurate—

can drive you and others crazy! We can drive others crazy even when we seek to develop relationships for the purpose of mutual benefit.

It is important, therefore, for us to spend time developing an understanding about the ups and downs of living life in our own skin. And coming to terms with how we interact with others who are important to the success of our individual business enterprises.

> Every participant should have taken the online personality profile BEFORE discussing the material about how your personality style impacts your entrepreneurial success.
>
> MyGreatPersonality.com

This is the website I designed for this workbook, giving a few options for determining your entrepreneur personality style (EPS). Hand yourself the gift of greater personal awareness. Do you want a quick "snapshot," or do you want the complete "photo album" of yourself? The more comprehensive, the better.

Understanding your personality is critical when trying to grasp how you deal with the ups and downs of relationships and also the way you approach your entrepreneurial pursuit. The personality model is a very important concept to grasp. It can and will provide a context for everything else in the book-workbook combination.

Taking the online personality profile (or the sixteen-page inventory, ordered through the same website) is an important component to this first emc^2 meeting. Understanding the information in the pages of your customized online personal profile report will also enhance your future business success, including the following issues:

- **PROBLEMS.** How you approach problems and challenges

- **PEOPLE.** How you interact and attempt to influence people

- **PACE.** How you respond to change and activities

- **PROCEDURE.** How you respond to rules set by others

IMPORTANT: At MyGreatPersonality.com there is also the ***Entrepreneur Attitude Assessment***, which identifies your personal strengths and vulnerabilities in the following six categories:

- Creativity

- Independence and Self-Reliance

DAY
1

What contributes most to your current life success? What part does gratitude play in your daily thoughts and actions?

DAY
2

What, if anything, is holding you back in your life? How do you know this to be true, and how are you going to deal with it?

DAY
3

What are your weakest job skills? How do you know this to be true?

DAY

4

What are your strongest job skills? How do you know this to be true?

DAY

5

List several of the most important goals in your life for the next year. List them in hierarchal order from the most to the least important. Attach a timeline for the accomplishment of each objective.

- Drive, Discipline, and Determination

- Energy

- Risk-Taking

- Communications

(Enter the code MYGP for the best discounts when ordering from mySimBiz or ruBizReady.)

More Resources: The comprehensive Freeman Institute® System One workbook (thirty-two pages) and personality profile (sixteen pages) are an excellent combination for every emc² member, providing practical, hands-on application to the DISC personality profile. Both can be ordered in any quantity from FreemanStuff.com.

Here's the simplified concept:
1. Discover the way you are wired—your entrepreneur personality style (EPS).
2. Be comfortable or become comfortable in your own skin.
3. Discover your passion(s) in life.
4. Go, do it—with a plan and an eternal purpose.

Discussion Questions from the Book and More:

1. When were you first bitten by the entrepreneurial bug? Share a brief version of that story with the rest of the group.

2. "We're all jockeys looking for a horse to ride." If this statement is true, part of the fun of living life on the edge is trying to discover the "horse" that God has designed specifically for each of us. In ten words or less, describe the "horse" God has given you to ride.

3. What have you learned about the strengths and vulnerabilities of your personality style as it relates to how you run your business? How would others close to you describe your personality style? How comfortable

are you with the view others may have of you? List the immediate areas of change, along with steps you can take to change.

Here are some thoughts to consider and/or discuss:

a.   What are your personal strengths? List them. Any strength, overused, can become a vulnerability. Being blunt is a wonderful strength. But is it possible to be too blunt? How can your strengths, overused, hinder your business success?

b.   Most folks come to work with pretty good intentions. People do not respond to intentions; they respond to behavior. Has there ever been a time when you were judged unfairly? As you reflect upon that incident, in what ways could your body language, tone, timing, or tact have added to the negative perceptions of the other person(s)? What wisdom lessons can be learned from that situation, enhancing the way you deal with your customers or associates?

c.   Seventy-five percent of personal development has to do with an internal view (thoughts, emotions, hot buttons, how we critique ourselves, etc.). The other 25 percent has to do with how we develop the necessary skills and tools to connect with the people around us (external view). What are your internal hot buttons? List them. Are there certain people and/or certain times of the week/month/year that make you more vulnerable to having those buttons pushed?

Develop a list of expectations you have of the emc^2 meetings. Also, make a list of the topics you'd like to have covered in future meetings, including some specific challenges you are experiencing in your particular business. Give both lists to the facilitator. Feel free to place your name and contact information on both lists.

THOUGHTS ON FINANCES AND THE BIBLE FROM A CERTIFIED FINANCIAL PLANNER™:

Check *Week One* in the appendix.

Prayer: "Lord, thank you for the way you designed me. Help me build upon my strengths and celebrate the way you made me. Help me identify my vulnerabilities and be aware of the ways I can keep them from becoming weaknesses. Show me ways to reach out beyond the comfort zones of my personality, becoming even more successful so that I can be a blessing to even more people."

A MOST FANTASTIC VIEW,
FOG PERMITTING

Ancient Wisdom

Proverbs 8:10–11: "Choose my instructions instead of silver, knowledge rather than choice gold, for wisdom is more precious than rubies, and nothing you desire can compare with her."

Proverbs 15:27: "A greedy man brings trouble to his family, but he who hates bribes will live."

Proverbs 16:3: "Commit to the LORD whatever you do, and your plans will succeed."

Reflections

As you read chapter one in the book, what were your initial thoughts and feelings about what you were reading (positive and/or negative)?

If you were able to communicate with the author while reading this chapter, what would you have said?

What were some thoughts (if any) you had about connecting the contents of this particular chapter to your business enterprise?

Additional Perspectives

In his excellent book *The War of Art*, Steven Pressfield states, "Most of us have two lives. The life we live, and the unlived life within us. Between the two stands *Resistance*. Have you ever brought home a treadmill and let it gather dust in the attic? Have you ever felt a call to embark upon a spiritual practice, dedicate yourself to a humanitarian calling, and commit your life to the service of others? Have you ever wanted to be a mother, a doctor, an advocate for the weak and helpless; to run for office, crusade for the planet, campaign for world peace, or preserve the environment? Late at night have you experienced a vision of the person you might become, the work you could accomplish, the realized being you were meant to be? Are you a writer who doesn't write, a painter who doesn't paint, an entrepreneur who never starts a venture? Then you know what Resistance is. . . . Resistance is the most toxic force on the planet. It is the root of more unhappiness than poverty, disease, and erectile dysfunction. To yield to Resistance deforms our spirit. It stunts us and makes us less than we are and were born to be. If you believe in God (and I do) you must declare Resistance evil, for it prevents us from achieving the life God intended when He endowed each of us with our own unique genius."

How do you and I respond to this thing Pressfield calls *Resistance*—the stuff that holds us back from fulfilling our dreams? How do you fight against personal laziness, inertia, rationalization, and procrastination? How does the theology of death, burial, and resurrection help us in experiencing the quality of life God intended for us?

Discussion Questions from Chapter One in the Book and More:

1. What is the vision and mission of your business? If you don't have a written mission statement, develop one. Write everything down, getting an even clearer image of the panoramic view before you. Even if you have a vision statement for your business, here are some personal questions that will help you focus:
    *   Why did I start this business enterprise?
    *   When I move on from this business, what do I want to leave behind? What's my legacy for the next generation(s)?
    *   What am I really providing for my clients beyond products and/or services?
    *   If money was no object and my business could be everything I dreamed, what would it be?

2. Describe and define the fog as it relates to your entrepreneurial pursuit. In other words, what makes you confused and perplexed, unclear about the next step(s) as you attempt to implement your vision and mission?

3. Joseph Conrad once stated, "It is not the clear-sighted who rule the world. Great achievements are accomplished in a blessed, warm fog." I suspect that no one reading this book is actually trying to rule the world, but what is your perspective on what this famous author is communicating, within the context of this book?

4. What are some advancing-through-the-fog strategies that can lead to "great achievements" when (not if) the thick fog settles in around you and your business pursuit? With pen in hand, identify specific practical concepts you can implement, addressing five layers. List at least one or

DAY

1

In terms of your career, where can you go from here? What are your options? Which option is the most viable? How will you get there?

DAY

2

What would your closest friend say are your hidden talents? (Take a guess.)

DAY

3

At a core level of yourself (soul), what are you trying to accomplish in your life?

DAY 4

What resides in the realm of your "shadow" (things you are trying to hide from yourself and others)? It has been said that to be alive is to be addicted in some way(s). If this is true, what are your socially acceptable and socially unacceptable addictions or habits, and how life controlling are they? In what specific ways? How much money do the addictions or habits you listed cost you on a daily, weekly, monthly, annual basis? Write those numbers down, and reflect on your response.

DAY 5

When was the last time you engaged in "impulse spending" of your limited energy on unscheduled activities? How often does something like this happen in your life?

two tactics per layer. Let's officially call it the "FERMS Fog Strategy" (try saying that fast five times!):

- **F**inancial

- **E**motional

- **R**elational

- **M**ental

- **S**piritual

THOUGHTS ON FINANCES AND THE BIBLE FROM A CERTIFIED FINANCIAL PLANNER™:

Check *Week Two* in the appendix.

Prayer: "Lord, please show me how I can spend my time wisely. Help me develop a set of statements that I can use for the rest of my life to keep my priorities straight. I want to be a person who mediates on your Word, maintaining an honest, open relationship with the Holy Spirit. Help me discern good in others and to genuinely love them with a sincere smile, a patient ear, and an affirming word."

DINNER AND A BOOK
THE IDEA FACTORY

Ancient Wisdom

Proverbs 11:25: "A generous man will prosper; he who refreshes others will himself be refreshed."

Proverbs 13:11: "Dishonest money dwindles away, but he who gathers money little by little makes it grow."

Proverbs 16:23: "A wise man's heart guides his mouth, and his lips promote instruction."

Reflections

As you read chapter two in the book, what were your initial thoughts and feelings about what you were reading (positive and/or negative)?

If you were able to communicate with the author while reading this chapter, what would you have said?

What were some thoughts (if any) you had about connecting the contents of this particular chapter to your business enterprise?

Additional Perspectives

Discovering the difference between a viable business dream and a nightmare.

Creative business dreams are generated by various sources (radio, newspapers, TV, etc.) and types (scientific, economic, political, etc.) of information. Once the idea starts to take shape, doing a SWOT analysis is absolutely vital. Once it passes the SWOT test, some business ideas are almost ready to be implemented. Website development helps to provide the public (digital) version of the business plan (BPI: business plan incognito) by forcing you to answer the five Ws and one H: who, what, when, where, why, and how.

The "Idea Factory" provides a visual overview of the process many business ideas go through before becoming ready for prime time. Creative ideas are all around us. These bright ideas pop into our minds at the oddest times: reading the newspaper; listening to two people complain about something while waiting in line at the grocery store; watching TV; surfing the Internet.

Regular market research, a feasibility study, and a business plan are very important if you want your business to expand. If the business opportunity is not feasible, you need to go back up to doing more market research to see if the plan really will work. If the business plan is not one that can be implemented, you will have to redo the business plan until it is fine-tuned.

But is the next idea you have a viable business dream or a nightmare? Is there a way to determine the difference? The "opportunity finding" process will help you discern the difference rather quickly. If your idea passes a thorough SWOT analysis you may be on the edge of something successful. Each new layer of the "Idea Factory" process will provide greater clarity and will bring you that much closer to the sweet smell of success in your business venture. It is worth the effort. Let's take a look on page 32:

IDEA FACTORY

Here is an example of how one person worked through the "Idea Factory" process:

She was a successful investment banker in a large city on the East Coast, working with wealthy clients. We'll call her Barbara. One day, one of her clients, a major league baseball player, was talking about his three dogs. He was in love with those dogs.

During the conversation he happened to mention that he hated cleaning up the dog doo-doo in his backyard. Barbara's ears perked up immediately, and she began asking questions. As someone who had never owned a pet, she learned more than she could have ever imagined about the smelly side of dog ownership.

Days went by, and Barbara couldn't shake off what she had heard. Her imagination went wild, thinking about the many dog owners in the region who had a similar hatred for picking up dog doo-doo. She did a SWOT analysis (see page 33 and also the information in chapter sixteen) and developed the beginnings of a business plan, trying to figure out the strengths, weaknesses, opportunities, and threats of starting such a business.

The next time she talked with the professional baseball player, Barbara casually asked him if he would be interested in paying someone to pick up the dog doo-doo in his backyard. His response was enthusiastic. He even started mentioning some names of other friends who might be interested in having someone come by on a regular basis providing a similar service. Her

Opportunity Finding: The "Idea Factory"

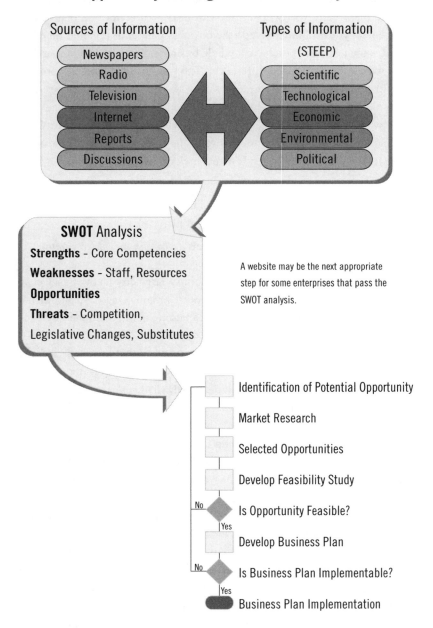

Sources of Information

- Newspapers
- Radio
- Television
- Internet
- Reports
- Discussions

Types of Information (STEEP)

- Scientific
- Technological
- Economic
- Environmental
- Political

SWOT Analysis

Strengths - Core Competencies

Weaknesses - Staff, Resources

Opportunities

Threats - Competition, Legislative Changes, Substitutes

A website may be the next appropriate step for some enterprises that pass the SWOT analysis.

- Identification of Potential Opportunity
- Market Research
- Selected Opportunities
- Develop Feasibility Study
- Is Opportunity Feasible? — No / Yes
- Develop Business Plan
- Is Business Plan Implementable? — No / Yes
- Business Plan Implementation

business was already starting to pick up (pun intended). She didn't leave her day job immediately.

Long story short, she drove in her sports car from house to house, two evenings a week, cleaning up the dog doo-doo. Her weekly income became so lucrative that she ultimately left her high-paying banking job to do it full time. And this was pre-Internet! No website. No email. No Twitter. No viral marketing. A grand accomplishment.

After several months she began hiring others to do most of the work, giving them a fair per-yard rate. Barbara grossed almost a million dollars her third year, with nine independent contractors working for her.

What kind of capital investment did she need to start a dog-doo-doo picking-up business? Less than a hundred bucks. A carton of plastic trash bags, gas for her sports car, a super-duper pooper-scooper, and some elbow grease.

STRENGTHS:

- Barbara was not afraid to start something new. Even though Barbara had an excellent investment banking job, she was open to new possibilities. Enjoying her job, with an open mind.

- Barbara was not afraid of looking like a fool. Someone might ask, "What kind of a job do you have?" Her response? "Oh, I pick up dog poop. My lifelong ambition realized. Ha ha ha . . ." (laughing all the way to the bank).

- Barbara had access to the people who could pay her high dollar for biweekly dog-doo-doo pickups.

- She had a wacky sense of humor that allowed her to do something like this, turning it into a fun business that made others laugh with her, not at her.

- The start-up capital was virtually nothing. No special vehicle was required. The only specialized tool was a super-duper pooper-scooper, readily available for fewer than thirty bucks.

- Barbara will be helping the environment. Officials nationwide have identified pet waste as a significant source of bacterial contamination and excess nutrients in lakes, rivers, and bays—

especially urban watersheds. Poop washes into waterways, creating health problems for swimmers who ingest the water. Pet poo also adds nitrogen to the water, which leads to algae blooms that suck up oxygen and kill fish.

WEAKNESSES:

Even though she had this wonderful sense of humor, she still had to confront her internal critic. "My parents paid all that money for me to finish school so that I could leave the safety and security of my 'real job' to become a dog doo-doo expert? I've got to be kidding myself. What kind of a career is this? Will it *really* work out for me, or am I following a crazy pipe dream? Wake up and smell the coffee, Barbara!"

OPPORTUNITIES:

- This could become a unique "human interest" story that would capture the imagination of local/regional/national newspapers, magazines, and TV shows. Can you imagine the headlines? "Business Picking Up for Investment Banker." "Woman's Business Going to the Dogs." "Banking on Dog Doo-Doo." "The Straight Poop on Business Success." You get the picture. Free, third-party endorsements and publicity. Her phone would ring off the hook.

- Ongoing marketing would mostly be word of mouth. Satisfied clients would talk at parties and other social occasions. "My dogs make the biggest messes in the backyard. That's the only thing I can't stand about my dogs. But you know what? I have found an incredibly funny woman—yes, a woman—to clean up the dog poo. You've got to meet Barbara. Let me tell you about her . . ."

- Barbara could make money only when she showed up. Hiring others to do the dirty work would free her up to market the business, would multiply her income, and would take the ceiling off her dream.

THREATS:

- As the word got out about her lucrative business venture, other copycats might try to muscle in on her territory by undercutting what she was charging. Since no one she knew of had ever started such an enterprise, she'd be doing the heavy lifting for opportunistic entrepreneurs looking to make an easy buck.

- Are there any environmental issues that she might have to deal with as more bags of dog doo-doo had to be dumped?

- Are there any legal liability issues she might have to confront?

- Hiring good help might be a problem. Should she do a background check on the people she was hiring? These individuals would be in the backyards of some pretty ritzy homes, with regular access. What if she inadvertently hired a thief who used his or her access to case the homes of wealthy people for burglaries later on?

Bottom Line: After careful analysis (SWOT analysis, business/financial/ marketing plans), Barbara reinvented herself. How did these new doors of opportunity open? On the hinges of a casual, conversational complaint from a client about cleaning up his pet's doo-doo. Keep alert. You never know what disguise opportunity will take on in your life.

I did a search on the Internet for any other similar businesses and immediately found a couple of enterprises on call. Is there a dog doo-doo business venture in your future?

How does the "Idea Factory" fit into your world?

Discussion Questions from Chapter Two in the Book and More:

1. In what ways is your counsel in demand? Identify those categories, writing them down on paper. How much time do you spend per month freely helping people in each category?

2. What are the ways you can free up yourself so that you can remain focused on the entrepreneurial things about which you are passionate— and still help people?

DAY
1

What is the most influential book you have ever read? List the ways that particular book changed your perspective on life, and send a thank-you note to the author if he or she is still alive.

DAY
2

Are you happy with your current lifestyle? Why or why not? What, if anything, have you determined needs to change?

DAY
3

Are you happy with your current family situation? Why or why not? If you are happy, how do you express your appreciation to those who love you? If you are unhappy, what will you do to change the situation?

DAY
4

What is your current spiritual practice, and is it
satisfying? Why or why not? If it is satisfying,
how do others around you know? If it isn't
satisfying, what steps will you take to change the
situation?

DAY
5

Explain the difference between efficient and
effective. Which term best describes your latest
business activities. Are you satisfied with the
chosen term?

3. "Of those who fail, most fail not realizing how close they were to success." I don't know the author, but what does this statement mean to you?

4. Any personal stories or experiences that you know of that can illustrate this quotation?

5. A dinner sponsored the idea for the book. What are the normal/ mundane things in your life that can spark a new idea?

6. Explain the "Idea Factory" concept, relating it to how you started your business or how you want to start your business.

7. What are the things you (or others) complain about the most? How can some of those complaints become the launching pad for an entrepreneurial venture (goods or services)?

8. What we say is important to our entrepreneurial success. Are you a person of your word? How careful are you about the words that come out of your mouth? When you make a statement, do you mean it? What is your definition of *integrity*? How does your definition of integrity correspond with the actual promises, guarantees and suggestions you make? Consider and discuss the concept of integrity and being a person of your word in light of the following real-life examples:

   i. "Let's do lunch real soon."
   ii. "I will call you next week."
   iii. "We ought to get together real soon."
   iv. "I will mail you that package tomorrow."
   v. "I will send you the information via email when I get back to my office."
   vi. "I will be there at 3:30."

   In other words, if you say you are going to do something—do it. If you say you're going to be somewhere—be there . . . a few minutes early. A big part of contributing to your future success is saying what you mean and following through.

THOUGHTS ON FINANCES AND THE BIBLE FROM A CERTIFIED FINANCIAL PLANNER™:

Check *Week Three* in the appendix.

Prayer: "Lord, help me see the opportunities that can spark a new business idea. Open up my eyes to see the topics where my counsel is in demand. I want to be a conduit of creativity and wisdom to many people, for your honor and for your glory."

DEATH OF A VISION

Ancient Wisdom

Proverbs 10:22: "The blessing of the LORD brings wealth, and he adds no trouble to it."

Proverbs 11:2: "When pride comes, then comes disgrace, but with humility comes wisdom."

Proverbs 13:20: "He who walks with the wise grows wise, but a companion of fools suffers harm."

Proverbs 15:16: "Better a little with the fear of the LORD than great wealth with turmoil."

Reflections

As you read chapter three in the book, what were your initial thoughts and feelings about what you were reading (positive and/or negative)?

If you were able to communicate with the author while reading this chapter, what would you have said?

What were some thoughts (if any) you had about connecting the contents of this particular chapter to your business enterprise?

Additional Perspectives

One entrepreneur has written:

Even though we were growing in spurts, my company almost died a few times. We've encountered so many obstacles, false hope, empty promises and dead ends. I've spent days and nights, wondering, thinking, brainstorming, banging my head against the wall and doing some good old-fashioned crying. The disappointments and challenges with the fund raising, with finding a development company/team, and with finding a way to make it happen tested and pushed me in ways I'd rather not think about any more. I picked up the saying 'Live and Learn' along the way, because that's the way it is. You live and you learn. You grow and you better yourself. The faster you adapt, you learn, and you grow, the quicker you make things happen. In my weakest moments, I have needed to have more strength then ever before in my life. The dream, the vision, and my passion are all I've had to pick me up and keep me going. I couldn't stop believing or wanting my company because it would die, and with it, would die my big chance to have an impact on the world. I couldn't survive that again. My former failed business had been enough. I believed the lessons I learned from that prepared me and set me up for success with my new venture. I tore myself to shreds to find ways to make it happen. I'm not proud of it, but I maxed out my credit cards, got behind on my mortgage payments, borrowed money from my dad, and counted on friends to help (my A/C broke and a friend replaced the entire system for me). It became an obsession and a matter of taking small steps forward in all the right directions: from networking with new people to getting involved in the right online communities. Sharing my pain, my sorrows, and my struggles helped a great deal; it brought about support from unexpected places and people. I kept making this venture my main priority. I didn't find success. I persevered until it found me. And it's still tough—almost every day.

These are not words written in the theoretical Business 101 classroom setting. They are etched in blood, sweat, and tears. A journal filled with hopes, fears, pain, and joy.

I conducted a talk show on the radio in the Baltimore/Washington region for eleven years. During this time, people would call with Bible questions, counseling needs, and other topics of interest.

If the caller took an extreme position on anything other than a primary doctrinal topic, I generally played the "devil's advocate" by reminding the caller that there were a number of Scriptures that could be legitimately interpreted to support an alternative view.

Hosting a radio talk show was a lot of fun—a wonderful laboratory for giving me the opportunity to step out of my narrow views on certain secondary teachings. Sometimes a caller would ask about the biblical perspective on prosperity, wealth, and success.

I enjoy discussing prosperity issues with Christians who use the Scriptures to support various schools of thought on the topic. There are extreme and moderate concepts. The extreme positions are easy to spot.

On the following pages are some Scriptures that might not be underlined or highlighted in the Bibles owned by people who may lean in the other direction. Please take the time to study them, remembering that the original language (Hebrew, Greek), historical background, and context (verses before and after) are important when trying to accurately interpret the meaning of any Bible verse.

A business vision is one of the more exciting events for an entrepreneur. Experiencing death of a vision is as predictable as the law of gravity. It's a necessary part of the process.

World Literature professor, David Allen White wrote, "Few of us, especially those of us who live comfortably in this artificial, cozy, comfortable, scientifically-fabricated world want to personally confront the idea and the reality of suffering. Not only Scripture, but the greatest writers of the past have in their greatest works given expression to the necessity of suffering—Sophocles in *Oedipus Rex*, Dante in the *Purgatorio*, Shakespeare in *King Lear*, Dostoevsky in *The Brothers Karamazov*, Solzhenitsyn in *The Gulag Archipelago*. The common theme—the necessity of suffering, for only through suffering may wisdom be attained, love fully understood, and the ways of God be made clear to us weak and erring creatures. Solzhenitsyn echoes Tolstoy by saying, 'Thank you, prison, for having been in my life.' We should be grateful for those sufferings sent to us; they are blessings. They are a way out of time and into eternity, a way out of self and into charity, a way out of sin and into salvation. As T. S. Eliot reminds us in the second of his *Four Quartets*, 'East Coker': '. . . In spite of that [suffering], we call this Friday good.'"

In light of this discussion I invite you to take a look at the Scriptures on this topic that you, perhaps, haven't underlined or highlighted in your Bible on either side of the topic.

There are a number of views of prosperity ranging from "the more prosperous and wealthy you are is an indication of your spirituality" to "possessing the bare minimum is a sign of God's blessing." What's even more intriguing is that both perspectives support their views with selected Scripture verses. Some people thrive on living a life of prosperity, while others seem to enjoy being knocked down and destitute. They seem to wear their suffering as a badge of honor.

On the following pages is a sample list of Scriptures that could be used to represent the extreme views:

Success/Prosperity/Wealth

Gen. 39:3 (Joseph) ". . . the LORD made all that he did to prosper in his hand." (NKJV)

Deut. 5:33 "Walk in all the way that the LORD your God has commanded you, so that you may live and prosper and prolong your days in the land that you will possess." (NKJV)

Deut. 28:1–2 "If you fully obey the LORD your God and carefully follow all his commands I give you today; the LORD your God will set you high above all the nations on earth. All these blessings will come upon you and accompany you if you obey the LORD your God." (NKJV)

Deut. 28:12 "The LORD will open the heavens, the storehouse of his bounty, to send rain on your land in season and to bless all the work of your hands. You will lend to many nations but you will borrow from none. The LORD will make you the head, not the tail . . . you will always be on top, never at the bottom." (NKJV)

Deut. 29:9 "Therefore keep the words of this covenant, and do them, that you may prosper in all you do." (NKJV)

Deut. 30:9 "Then the LORD your God will make you most prosperous in all the work of your hands and in the fruit of your womb, the young of your livestock and the crops of your land. The LORD will

Persecution/Suffering/Poverty

Prov. 11:28 "Whoever trusts in his riches will fall . . ." (NKJV)

Prov. 23:4 "Do not wear yourself out to get rich; have the wisdom to show restraint."

Matt. 5:3 "Blessed are the poor (*ptokos*, destitute) in spirit for theirs is the kingdom of heaven."

Matt. 6:19 "Do not store up for yourselves treasures on earth, where moth and rust destroy, and where thieves break in and steal."

Matt. 6:24 "You cannot serve God and Money."

Matthew 6:25–32 "Therefore I tell you, do not worry about your life, what you eat or drink; or about your body, what you will wear. Is not life more important than food . . . than clothes? Look at the birds of the air; they do not sow or reap or store away in barns, and yet your heavenly Father feeds them. Are you not much more valuable than they? Who of you by worrying can add a single hour to his life? And why do you worry about clothes? See how the lilies of the field grow. They do not labor or spin. Yet I tell you that not even Solomon in all his splendor was dressed like one of these . . . O you of little faith? So do not worry, saying 'What shall we eat?' or 'What shall we drink?' or 'What shall we wear?' For the pagans run after these things, and your heavenly Father knows that you need them."

Success/Prosperity/Wealth

again delight in you and make you prosperous . . ."

1 Chron. 22:13 (Solomon) ". . . then you will prosper, if you take heed to fulfill . . ." (NKJV)

2 Chron. 26:5 (Zechariah) ". . . as long as he sought the Lord, God made him prosper. (NKJV)

2 Chron. 31:21 (Hezekiah) ". . . to seek his God, he did it with all his heart. So he prospered." (NKJV)

Neh. 2:20 (Nehemiah) ". . . the God of heaven Himself will prosper us . . ." (NKJV)

Job 36:11 "If they obey and serve him, they will spend the rest of their days in prosperity and their years in contentment."

Ps. 1:1–3 "Blessed is the man who does not walk in the counsel of the wicked or stand in the way of sinners or sit in the seat of mockers. But his delight is in the law of the LORD, and on his law he meditates day and night. He is like a tree planted by streams of water, which yields its fruit in season and whose leaf does not wither. Whatever he does prospers."

Ps. 122:6 "Pray for the peace of Jerusalem: may they prosper who love you." (NKJV)

Ps. 128:2 "You will eat the fruit of your labor, blessings and prosperity will be yours."

Prov. 3:1–5 ". . . do not forget my teaching . . . for they will prolong your life many years and bring

Persecution/Suffering/Poverty

John 15:20 (Jesus) ". . . No servant is greater than his master. If they persecuted me, they will persecute you also . . ."

Acts 9:16 (Paul) "I will show him how much he must suffer for my name."

Rom. 8:18 "I consider that our present sufferings are not worth comparing with the glory that will be revealed in us."

2 Cor. 11:23–31 (Paul) ". . . Three times I was beaten with rods, . . . three times I was shipwrecked . . . I have been constantly on the move. I have been in danger . . . I have labored and toiled and have often gone without sleep: I have known hunger and thirst and have often gone without food; I have been cold and naked . . . If I must boast, I will boast of the things that show my weakness . . ."

Phil. 3:7–10 "But whatever was to my profit I now consider loss for the sake of Christ. What is more, I consider everything a loss compared to the surpassing greatness of knowing Christ Jesus my Lord, for whose sake I have lost all things. I consider them rubbish, that I may gain Christ . . . I want to know Christ and the power of his resurrection and the fellowship of sharing in his sufferings, becoming like him in his death."

Heb. 13:5 "Keep your lives free from the love of money and be content with what you have . . ."

Success/Prosperity/Wealth

you prosperity. Let love and faithfulness never leave you . . . Then you will win favor and a good name in the sight of God and man. Trust in the LORD with all your heart and lean not on your own understanding; in all your ways acknowledge him, and he will make your paths straight."

Prov. 8:32–35 ". . . listen to me; blessed are those who keep my ways. . . . Blessed is the man who listens to me . . . for whoever finds me finds life and receives favor from the LORD."

Prov. 21:21 "He who pursues righteousness and love finds life, prosperity and honor."

Matt. 6:33–34 "But seek first his kingdom and his righteousness, and all these things will be given to you as well."

Mark 11:24 "Therefore, I tell you, whatever you ask for in prayer, believe that you have received it, and it will be yours."

Luke 6:38 "Give, and it will be given you. A good measure, pressed down, shaken together and running over . . ."

3 John 2 "Beloved, I wish above all things that you prosper and be in health, even as thy soul prospers." (KJV)

* There are many more that could have been added to this list . . .

Persecution/Suffering/Poverty

1 Tim. 6:5–19 ". . . men of corrupt mind . . . who think that godliness is a means to financial gain. But godliness with contentment is great gain. For we brought nothing into this world, and we certainly can bring nothing out of it. But if we have food and clothing, we will be content with that. People who want to get rich fall into temptation and a trap and into many foolish and harmful desires that plunge men into ruin and destruction. For the love of money is a root of all kinds of evil. Some people eager for money, have wandered from the faith and pierced themselves with many griefs. . . . Command those who are rich in this present world not to be arrogant nor to put their hope in wealth, which is so uncertain, but to put their hope in God, who richly provides us with everything for our enjoyment. Command them to do good, to be rich in good deeds, and to be generous and willing to share. In this way they will lay up treasures for themselves as a firm foundation for the coming age . . ."

2 Tim. 3:12 ". . . all that will live godly in Christ Jesus shall suffer persecution." (KJV)

* There are many more that could have been added to this list . . .

Prosperity and Suffering/Poverty Combined

Psalm 62:9–10 "Lowborn men are but a breath, the highborn are but a lie; if weighed on a balance, they are nothing . . . though your riches increase, do not set your heart on them."

Proverbs 30:8 ". . . give me neither poverty nor riches, but give me only my daily bread."

Ecclesiastes 3:1–8 "There is a time for everything and a season for every activity under heaven: a time to be born and a time to die, a time to plant and a time to uproot . . . a time to tear down and a time to build, a time to weep and a time to laugh, a time to mourn and a time to dance . . . a time to search and a time to give up, a time to keep and a time to throw away, a time to tear and a time to mend. . . ."

Ecclesiastes 11:8 "However many years a man may live, let him enjoy them all. But let him remember the days of darkness, for they will be many. . . ."

Mark 10:29–30 "I tell you the truth," Jesus replied, "no one who has left home or brothers or sisters or mother or father or children or fields for me and the gospel will fail to receive a hundred times as much in this present age (homes, brothers, sisters, mothers, children and fields—and with them, persecution). . . ."

Phil. 4:11–12 ". . . for I have learned to be content whatever the circumstances. I know what it is to be in need, and I know what it is to have plenty. I have learned the secret of being content in any and every situation, whether well fed or hungry. . . ."

I have performed funerals of many people from all walks of life. The great leveler of us all is found in the words of Job, "Naked I came from my mother's womb, and naked I will depart."

I have talked with some folks who believe that every Christian is to be wealthy. Some believe that we should be driving the most expensive automobiles, always healthy, never making a "negative confession," wearing the finest clothing, and dwelling in architectural splendor. Also known as "Prosperity Doctrine," "Health and Wealth," "Name It and Claim It," or "Blab It and Grab It." (The terms tend to be used by those who criticize this teaching.)

Personal Observation: Having traveled extensively around the world, I always wonder why the "wealth and health gospel" perspective seems so hollow when I am invited in to eat and/or fellowship with a believer in a developing nation who makes the equivalent of five hundred dollars a year. I realize very quickly that this individual is experiencing a wealth of prayer, genuine humility, love, and contentment that I cannot begin to touch with my North American consciousness. Some of the greatest personal life lessons have emerged from such encounters. It begs the question: What is authentic success in God's eyes?

Others I have talked with believe that Christians shouldn't strive for wealth, and if they are financially well off, they shouldn't flaunt it with displays of fine cars and homes. Poverty is viewed by some as a sign of spiritual depth and godly maturity. This world is not our home, and we shouldn't live like it is. We are strangers, foreigners, and pilgrims, just passing through to our eternal home with streets paved with gold. ("Worm Theology" is a term used by some who criticize this teaching.) Expressions of low self-worth mean that God is more likely to show compassion and mercy.

A background: "Worm Theology" comes from David (Psalm 22:6) and Job (Job 17:14; 25:6—Bildad) viewing themselves as worms, Jacob being viewed as a worm (Isaiah 41:14), and also from a line in the Isaac Watts hymn "Alas! And Did My Savior Bleed," which says, "Would He devote that sacred head for such a worm as I?" When this hymn was originally written (early 1700s), it was believed by some that all humans were as worms in the dirt and in despair of personal sin.

Personal Observation: I always wonder why people who view poverty and suffering as a sign of spirituality like to reach out to wealthy people when there is a financial need for their ministry and then praise the Lord for the provision of funds that arrived "just in time at the eleventh hour." I have seen too much of the "love of money" and the "catering to the wealthy" oozing from people who don't have it and are proud of their no-extra-cash station in life.

In light of these thoughts, consider the following statement: "Where there is no business (real-world finances to take care of bills), there is no ministry (the ability to reach out to others from a position of strength)." How we view the use of finances must be an important issue, since over 60 percent of the parables taught by Jesus were about money.

The various extreme views seem to either disregard or explain away each other's position. More heat than light. I have personal convictions, but I am not going to try to convince anyone of my views in this forum. I am hoping that the way I am presenting the information will spark deep thought, biblical research, and healthy discussions.

Perhaps the balanced, biblical view is somewhere between the two extremes. What are you thinking about this topic at this moment?

In his article "What Is Money?" Ronald Nash has given us his studied perspective:

> Jesus often spoke about wealth without condemning it (Matthew 13:44–46; 21:33–46). When he did call on people to renounce their possessions, his statements reflected special conditions; in one instance, for example, he made this demand in a situation where people had made their possessions into a god (Luke 18:22–24). Instead of condemning wealth then, Jesus' teaching offered an important perspective on how people living in materialistic surroundings should view the material world. What Jesus condemned was not wealth per se, but the improper acquisition and use of wealth. Every Christian, rich or poor, needs to recognize that whatever he or she possesses is theirs temporarily as a steward under God. Wealth that is accumulated dishonestly or that becomes a controlling principle in one's life falls under God's judgment. Wealth resulting from honest labor and wise investment, wealth that is handled by people who recognize their role as stewards under God does not. Those who draw attention only to passages in which Jesus indicted prosperous people are presenting only part of his teaching. Jesus also praised those who through wise management and careful stewardship created wealth. We must avoid the temptation of selecting a few passages from the Gospels and attempting to show that Jesus' views conformed to our preferred opinions and lifestyle. Jesus' teaching about money, wealth, and poverty is extremely diverse.

Do you agree with Nash? Why or why not? What research process informs your study of the Bible on this or any other topic? Here are two definitions that may help you determine the way you develop personal, biblically based convictions.

Exegesis: The critical explanation or interpretation of Scripture, searching to determine the truth it presents and expresses to develop a doctrine, belief, or explanation. Taking out of the text what is there.

Eisegesis: An interpretation, especially of Scripture, that reflects the personal ideas, bias, or viewpoint of the interpreter, rather than the meaning of the text; reading something into a text that isn't there. To take a position and then to seek support to prove it typically leads to putting into or reading into the text what is not really there. Having a thought or theory and digging through Scripture to find evidence to support it.

Some people pull a verse out of the Bible to support a particular point of view. But that raises a lot of questions. Who wrote it? To whom was it written? Why was it written? What are some of the linguistic hints from the original language?

It is always a good exercise to look at the verses before and after to get a context for that verse. An understanding of the original language will help, along with an awareness of the historical ramifications surrounding that part of the Bible.

What are your views about prosperity and success? Do you have a predetermined (eisegetical) view, looking for Scripture verses to support it? Or does your perspective on this topic emerge from careful study (exegetical), allowing the whole counsel of the Scriptures to shape your thinking on this matter?

What is the bottom-line purpose of financial wealth and health?

What is the bottom-line purpose of pain and suffering?

Take a look at the chronology of two major events in Jesus' life—death and resurrection. Then take a look at two major events in the life of his disciples—the cross preceded Pentecost. As modern-day disciples of Jesus, most love the excitement of Pentecost but hate the pain and confusion surrounding death at the cross. What kind of parallel is there to what you have experienced or are experiencing in your business life? Does death seem to precede resurrection even in the business world? If not, why? If so, how?

DAY

1

What do you do to renew and regenerate yourself?
How often do you do this? List three ways (even
if small ones) in which you can create and use
leisure time in your life right now.

DAY

2

What is your vision of yourself in five to ten years
from now? Why is this your particular vision?
How will you achieve it?

DAY

3

What did people used to say you could be?

DAY 4

Other than your spouse, who is your closest friend, and how long have you been friends? How often do you interact with him or her, and in what ways does your friend positively impact you? In what ways do you positively impact your friend?

DAY 5

How would you explain the importance of Christ's resurrection in your life?

Discussion Questions from Chapter Three in the Book and More:

1. What drives you, truly motivates you—beyond a paycheck?

2. What is your death-of-a-vision story? Have you ever written it down? If not, do what you can to write the main elements of your story.

3. What wisdom lessons have you learned from that period in your life?

4. How are you passing these wisdom lessons on to the next generation?

5. Is there a difference between *riches* and *wealth*? If so, what is it? Does *rich* include anything more than money and the accumulation of stuff in the here and now? How does *wealth* relate to your relationships, family, morals, and values that last for eternity? How many more aspects can you list when thinking about *wealth*? Write your definition of both words, and determine what you are personally committed to: *riches* and/or *wealth*? Is it possible to have one and not the other? Why or why not?

6. Someone once said, "There is an occupational hazard to becoming wealthy. The more wealth we accumulate, the more tempted we are to become independent of God." Discuss this statement, giving reasons as to why you agree or disagree with this statement.

7. Read the eighth chapter of Deuteronomy (especially vv. 17–18). Then read the tenth chapter of 1 Corinthians (especially vv. 11–13). Discuss (and write down) the parallels between the history of Israel and how individuals sometimes get seduced by the accumulation of wealth.

8. Discuss the implications of a statement made by Will Smith: "Money and success don't change people; they merely amplify what is already there." What personal examples or other people's experiences can you share that will help to understand what Will is communicating?

9. Try to make sense of statements like:

- "I have worked my fingers to the bone."
  (Who gave you the fingers and the bones?)

- "I did this job by the sweat of my brow."
  (Who gave you the brow that sweats?)

- "I thought of that creative business idea."
  (Who gave you the mind that thinks?)

- "I have earned my own money."
  (Are you the *owner* or an *administrator* of that money? Define and then discuss the difference between the two words "owner" and "administrator.")

10. Read John 15 (entire chapter). Focus on verse 5: "Apart from me you can do nothing." List all of your gifts, skills, and strengths as a businessperson, and then discuss the fine line between your God-given skills/talents and your choices as a human being and his gift of temporal/eternal life, redemption, and power. Factor in the reality that you are a created being. Everything in your body and intellect is a gift from God Almighty. Celebrate this reality in a fresh, new way. Enter into a new way of worshiping our Creator.

11. How significant is the presence of the Holy Spirit in your everyday life? If the Holy Spirit wasn't in your life, would others notice any changes in the way you conduct your life? If so, what changes would they notice? How can you better connect with the Holy Spirit alive and at work in you?

12. Wrestle with a familiar question: If you were arrested for being a Christian, would there be enough evidence to convict you? If so, discuss the evidence. If not, why not?

THOUGHTS ON FINANCES AND THE BIBLE FROM A CERTIFIED FINANCIAL PLANNER™:

Check *Week Four* in the appendix.

Prayer: "Lord, many people seem to pass the test of persecution, pain, and suffering; but very few individuals, and fewer nations, have been able to pass the test of prosperity, success, and wealth. I am willing to be tested with prosperity, and I will work toward that end. But, Lord, you know what I can handle. Open doors that I cannot shut and shut doors that I cannot open. I will do my part, and I thank you for doing your part. I trust you, even when I am experiencing death to the business dream(s)."

DESIGNING YOUR FUTURE

Ancient Wisdom

Proverbs 11:24: "One man gives freely, yet gains even more; another withholds unduly, but comes to poverty."

Proverbs 19:17: "He who is kind to the poor lends to the LORD, and he will reward him for what he has done."

Proverbs 22:1–2: "A good name is more desirable than great riches. . . . Rich and poor have this in common: The LORD is the Maker of them all."

Reflections

As you read chapter four in the book, what were your initial thoughts and feelings about what you were reading (positive and/or negative)?

If you were able to communicate with the author while reading this chapter, what would you have said?

What were some thoughts (if any) you had about connecting the contents of this particular chapter to your business enterprise?

Additional Perspectives

In the circle below, place examples of the things/experiences that are in your personal comfort zone inside the circle. Place all of the things/experiences that are outside of your comfort zone outside the circle.

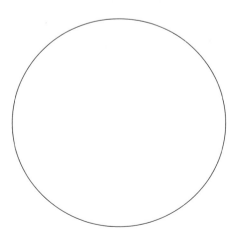

Here are some idea starters, which may be inside or outside the circle: presenting your business plan to a complete stranger, traveling to an unknown destination by yourself, expressing your true negative feelings to a business partner, doing detailed research for your business or marketing plan, dealing with conflict, talking on the telephone with a potential client, using email, learning how to build a website, standing up in front of a group of people and speaking for thirty minutes, asking for help from a member of your family, raising money for a project, making an expense report (with receipts) for your accountant, and/or learning to play golf. These concepts will get you started, helping you come up with items that are relevant to you and your life.

COMFORT ZONE

Pushing yourself outside your comfort zone may be one of the greatest keys to your business and relationship success. Perhaps this exercise will give you some ideas. The items outside the circle can become the focus of your personal development for the rest of your life.

How does God's plan for your life push you outside of your comfort zone?

List the ways your business causes you to stretch in the following categories:

Personally:

Professionally:

Mentally:

Emotionally:

Spiritually:

Physically:

Financially:

Relationally:

DAY 1

If you had to follow some other line of work, what might it be? What is it about this line of work that would draw you? What are the barriers to following this type of work? Is it worth it to you to put your effort and passion into smashing through those barriers?

DAY 2

If you have ever had a peak experience, what was it, and how did it positively impact your life?

DAY
3

Who in your family are you least alike? List the attributes and how this has affected you.

DAY
4

Who in your family are you the most alike? List the attributes and how this has affected you.

DAY
5

To what extent do you feel that your priorities need to be reordered at this point in your life?

Discussion Questions from Chapter Four in the Book and More:

1. If you are resistant to the concepts outlined in this chapter, what are the excuses about web development ricocheting around in your brain? Make a list of those excuses.

2. How will you respond to each excuse?

3. If you already do your own web work, what is your philosophy about design and maintenance of a website? If you already have a website, what changes, if any, will you make to your website?

4. How many web design commandments can you come up with? That, by the way, just might be the beginnings of a booklet you will publish.

5. Sit down for about an hour, writing on a separate sheet of paper all of the domain names you would like to own—expanding your digital real estate holdings. Be creative, letting the ideas flow. At MultiWebConcepts.com there is a search engine designed to determine if a website domain name you want has been taken or not. Go there with the domain names on your list, and follow the directions. You will soon become a digital real estate mogul.

6. What kind of a website can you develop that can be used exclusively for some type of ministry outreach?

7. List the three most challenging areas of your life that are outside of your comfort zone. What are you going to do about them? What kind of timeline are you going to impose upon yourself to address these aspects of your life?

THOUGHTS ON FINANCES AND THE BIBLE FROM A CERTIFIED FINANCIAL PLANNER™:

Check *Week Five* in the appendix.

Prayer: "Lord, help me apply your spiritual counsel and wisdom in my daily life. Guide me with your Word and your Spirit. Help me use the available technology to reach out to as many people as I possibly can. Thank you for allowing me to have an eternal purpose . . . especially with the way I utilize my finances."

BRANDING YOURSELF

Ancient Wisdom

Proverbs 11:28: "Whoever trusts in his riches will fall, but the righteous will thrive like a green leaf."

Proverbs 15:33: "The fear of the LORD teaches a man wisdom, and humility comes before honor."

Proverbs 19:8: "He who gets wisdom loves his own soul; he who cherishes understanding prospers."

Reflections

As you read chapter five in the book, what were your initial thoughts and feelings about what you were reading (positive and/or negative)?

If you were able to communicate with the author while reading this chapter, what would you have said?

What were some thoughts (if any) you had about connecting the contents of this particular chapter to your business enterprise?

Additional Perspectives

The *good* is the enemy of the *best*. The more talented you are, the more opportunities will come your way. You need to be discerning about how you extend yourself. One of the best ways to determine how to expend your time and energy is to develop a *Life Vision Statement* and *a Life Mission Statement*. You can then drill down, developing your *Core Values Statement*.

I was reticent about including my very personal statements in this book. These are private, personally meaningful statements. After careful consideration and prayer I decided to include them to stir up your own thinking on this topic. The following statements are a part of this workbook as an example of how one person has done it. You will want to develop your own statements that will reflect what's important to you.

Life Vision Statement of Joel A. Freeman
"To glorify Jesus Christ with every fiber of my being
—in season and out of season."

Life Mission Statement of Joel A. Freeman

"I will continue to joyfully study the art of public speaking, coaching, and writing so that I can be a transparent vehicle to encourage people of all shapes, colors, ages, and status to take a brand new look at Jesus Christ. My relationships with my wife, family, and friends are the litmus test of my success. In all this, I will always have a burning passion to be involved in world missions in some way, with a special emphasis on communicating Christ with agnostics, atheists, cynics, and skeptics."

Core Values of Joel A. Freeman

"I will keep an honest, open relationship with the Holy Spirit, repenting when personal sin is revealed. By God's grace, I will be a man of integrity before God (vertical) and people (horizontal). If I have offended someone or have been offended by someone, I will go to that person alone, seeking healing for our relationship, regardless of the potential outcome. Success and failure are both treated as imposters. I will deal honestly with people. Truthful. Just. Genuinely interested in people regardless of their station in life. Kind. Generous. Living in the present, while thankful for the past and hopeful about the future. I want to be known as a man who loves and studies the Word of God. A reader of books that span both time and subject matter. Constantly motivated by curiosity. Faithful to my wife. Grace-oriented in all relationships. The knowledge of heaven and eternity establishes a foundation from which I develop my core values, make present-day decisions, and initiate goals."

Life Mottoes of Joel A. Freeman

"Let's continue to keep the eternal perspective in clear view."

"Let's continue to keep our hearts tender toward Jesus—ALWAYS!"

"Do the details with dignity."

"God is my audience."

"Do first what you dread the most."

"Work hard. Work smart. Enjoy the journey."

"Start things worth finishing and then finish what you start."

"The instant I meet Jesus face to face, I will wish that I was bolder about my faith while I was living on earth."

"Seek first to understand before seeking to be understood."

"We are not human beings having a spiritual experience. We are spiritual beings having a human experience."

Take the time—perhaps an entire weekend—to develop your personal Life Vision, Life Mission, and Core Value statements. You may even want to identify some Life Motto statements that have meant a lot to you. Statements worth embroidering.

Make a copy of all statements, frame them, and then place them near your workstation. Reflect upon them often. I keep a copy in my wallet and often reevaluate my life in relationship to these statements. When stuck in airports on flight connections or weather-related layovers, I find plenty of time for such healthy introspection.

I hope the inclusion of my statements will provide the necessary catalyst for you to develop your own statements—and then to live by them. This kind of personal reflection will positively affect the success of your business in more ways than I could ever communicate in this workbook. A kind of a spiritual GPS. It might even impact what matters a million years from now.

Below is the prayer that I often say to the Lord. Read Psalm 111 first, and then you will understand the context for Psalm 112 (read it also), the basis for this prayer:

> *"Dear Lord, I worship you for who you are and praise you for what you do. My desire is to trust and respect you in all things and to delight in the things that you require of me. Remind me that living a righteous life is not an event; it is the essence of the journey. May my children (pray for each child by name) be mighty warriors who are a blessing to their generation. Give me creative business ideas that will bring wealth and riches to my home so that we can freely and quietly bless others who are serving you throughout the world, generously helping as many people as possible who are in need. Help me to be a gracious and compassionate man. May people remember me as a man filled with integrity, conducting my affairs with justice for all. Secure and joyful, living life on the edge without the fear of bad news. Help me to be a man who is not shaken by negative circumstances. May I out love all of my enemies and outlive all of my critics. May I accomplish much in your name, so that you will be glorified. If you lift my gifts and talents to honorable places, may I always internally recognize and remember that you are the one who is the Giver of everything. Regardless what happens throughout my life, I give you all the honor, the glory, and the praise."*

It's all about God.

Discussion Questions from Chapter Five in the Book and More:

1. Using a thesaurus, pick out action words that describe the vision and mission of your entrepreneurial pursuit. These words will get the creative juices flowing.

DAY
1

Name two things that repel you. Why? How do these things affect your life?

DAY
2

Name two things you are strongly attracted to. Why? How do these things affect your life?

DAY
3

Have there ever been any unexplainable events in your life? Name them, expressing their impact upon you.

DAY

4

Name something that energizes you. In what way(s)? And when was the last time you experienced it?

DAY

5

To what extent are you living in the past (guilt) or future (fear) in some area of your life? How does this rob you of living in the present?

2. How can you channel your unique skill sets and brain trust of experience into an identifiable brand? Develop a series of brief statements that might be finalists in your quest for a brand. Let yourself go. Look for something that reflects your personality. Nothing is too crazy to put on paper. Bounce the ideas off the creative people who love you and celebrate you.

3. What was Jesus' main message? What was his vision and mission while on earth? I do not want this to sound weird or even sacrilegious, but if you were called on to develop Jesus' brand for his three-year public ministry on earth, what would it communicate? (Here's a starter idea: S³ *"Seeking and Saving Sinners."*) Can you think of a better brand? What is the branding statement for your personal vision and mission?

THOUGHTS ON FINANCES AND THE BIBLE FROM A CERTIFIED FINANCIAL PLANNER™:

Check *Week Six* in the appendix.

Prayer: "Lord, your Word states that I am an heir of your kingdom. I am a coheir with Jesus because of his death on Calvary. The bounty of your kingdom is available to me, and I go forward into this day knowing that your future for me in your kingdom is greater than my highest dreams. This is a gift I cannot ever earn or deserve. It's all because of your grace and mercy. Like the one man who returned to express his thanks for being healed from leprosy, I am grateful."

MARKETING YOURSELF

Ancient Wisdom

Proverbs 15:22: "Plans fail for lack of counsel, but with many advisers they succeed."

Proverbs 16:7: "When a man's ways are pleasing to the LORD, he makes even his enemies live at peace with him."

Proverbs 28:19: "He who works his land will have abundant food, but the one who chases fantasies will have his fill of poverty."

Reflections

As you read chapter six in the book, what were your initial thoughts and feelings about what you were reading (positive and/or negative)?

If you were able to communicate with the author while reading this chapter, what would you have said?

What were some thoughts (if any) you had about connecting the contents of this particular chapter to your business enterprise?

Additional Perspectives

Most entrepreneurs do not necessarily fear failure. They fear not trying a potentially viable business venture. (This concept was briefly mentioned in the first session about different personalities.) You have to have a big ego/confidence to believe that you can accomplish what relatively few others have done in the business world.

What does a typical workday look like for you? How do your pride and ego impact the way you function and how you deal with people?

Here is one person's story. She is an entrepreneur struggling with the normal stuff many people experience. Even though she is self-employed, her new business involves training and working with other people—kind of like someone working in real estate:

> I've been working for myself—setting my own hours, setting the pace, and only answering to me. It's been difficult at times and at times very boring, but to be honest, being self-employed is the only option for me.
>
> On Thursday, I went in for some training and briefings. I came home that evening, after being stuck in traffic, completely exhausted. The entire day involved dealing with more emotions

related to the whole situation I'm in and I realized how much my ego and pride were key players to me feeling bruised, hurt, discontent, out of place, and under new constraints.

Everyone is fabulous and wonderful and the new job is, indeed, a perfect fit—the way I feel has nothing to do with that. It has everything to do with me. I am currently not where I imagined myself to be in life. I have fallen short of my expectations, my desires, and my goals. I can't think nor see myself as just someone who works for someone else. I can't have others see me or think of me that way either. I really thought that by now, I would be further along in building my own empire.

About two weeks ago, I went out to dinner with someone I met online. After explaining to him what I was doing for a job, he replied: "So you're unemployed?" I wanted to cuss at him and get up and leave. I then realized, of course, that he was just calling it the way he saw it. I replied with: "You're obviously not a visionary." But his comment, unfortunately, stayed with me and it took me a few days to digest it.

I know what I'm capable of doing and yet, it's not happening. I've been brewing on this a lot more. I understand that there is no value in our ego or in our pride. Neither one is useful when it comes to reaching real happiness, contentment, or spiritual growth. My worth, my confidence, and who I am are not rooted in what I do, accomplish, or possess, but guess what—I'm HUMAN. My ego and pride do come out and play—they do drive me to perform better, to achieve more, and to reach higher levels of success. I think BIG and I want BIG things to happen in my life and for my life.

I'm a little (as in very) ticked off that I'm not where I want to be and I'm determined to turn up the heat and get there.

In what ways can you relate to this person's experience? In what ways can you cast a spiritual light on dealing with your ego? If the word "ego" stands for "edging God out," when was the last time you edged God out of your life? What wisdom lessons have you learned from that experience?

Ultimately we must focus on Christ: preaching Christ crucified and living Christ crucified. It's not about us, our businesses, or our churches. It's all about him. Jesus draws people to himself and grows his church—not us! We must celebrate those who come to Jesus and walk with Jesus, but it should be a celebration of his grace and mercy and not of our own works.

How do you know when your business efforts are in concert with the eternal perspective? Give a recent example of this knowledge about the way the eternal perspective has positively impacted your life.

BONUS PERSPECTIVE: The Push and Pull of the Market

To get business, we often talk about a "push vs. pull strategy" in marketing. Do you "push" your idea out to people, telling them about it, sending out lots of advertising, etc. Or is your business idea so strong and so creative that the market "pulls" at you, wanting your goods or services. Do you "pull" them into your business with enticing offers based on their felt needs?

It might be good to take a long look at what you do and then determine which aspects of your business you will need to "push" into the marketplace and which aspects are so innovative that the marketplace will "pull" on you for your goods or services.

There may be a time for both strategies at various stages of growth in your business enterprise. Sometimes a small "push" will deliver a huge "pull." And sometimes your business idea is so creative that you need to commit yourself to a long-term "push" to give the public a chance to "pull" it from you. The "Idea Factory" (covered in week three) will help you determine whether or not you have an idea that is worthy of a long-term "push" to get the kind of market "pull" that will reward your effort handsomely. Let's take a step back in time to better grasp these concepts.

If you were born before 1960, you were probably quite grumpy when you purchased your first CD player. You may have felt you were being "pushed" into purchasing a product that you didn't ask for or desire. If this was your reaction, you weren't alone. I was grumpy right there with you, especially since I had just spent some hard-earned cash on a fine turntable! Like me, the world music conglomerates were so heavily invested in the multi-billion-dollar LP analog record technology that initially they weren't even interested in digital technology. Let's take a look at how the digital revolution illustrates market "pull."

According to the official written history of the advancement of digital technology at Sony (entire history found at Sony.net), "Heitaro Nakajima is a communications engineer best known for his pioneering work on digital recording at the NHK and at Sony Corporation. In 1971 Heitaro resigned from his post as head of NHK's Technical Research Laboratories and joined Sony. Four years earlier at NHK, Nakajima had commenced work on the digitization of sound and within two years had developed the first digital audio tape recorder."

Sony history goes on to inform that "Nakajima, unable to forget the first time he heard digital sound, did not give up," even though there were some major setbacks and negativity within the Sony Corporation toward his research. "He earnestly believed that digital technology would be valuable in the future. Ten years after he started his research, he still held the belief that 'digital technology would be valuable within ten years.' Achieving the best sound quality was his lifelong dream."

Here's an overview of how the marketplace "pulled" for digital technology after Sony had "pushed" it on us. It didn't take long. Let's take a glimpse into a ten-year period—a decade of incredible global change:

- **1982**—First digital audio 5-inch CD discs marketed, merging the consumer music industry with the computer revolution.

- **1984**—The increase in production quantities of CD titles in Japan over the years is proof of the speed with which this technology caught on. The number of CDs produced was a mere one-tenth the number of LPs.

- **1986**—Just four years later, CD production rose to 45 million per year, far outstripping LP production.

- **1988**—The CD became the principal audio medium in a relatively short time after its introduction. 100 million CDs were being produced annually, matching the quantity for LPs at their peak. For the first time, CD sales surpassed LP sales, making CD and cassette as the two dominant consumer formats; more than half of TV households own a VCR; the first transatlantic fiber-optic cable carried up to 37,000 telephone transmissions and began to replace satellites for telephone communication.

- **1990**—28 percent of all U.S. households have CDs. 9.2 million players sold annually in the United States. 288 million CDs sold annually in the United States. World sales close to 1 billion.

- **1992**—CD production tripled to 300 million a year.

Technology Timeline Information © 1999-2004 by Steven E. Schoenherr. All rights reserved. Found on http://history.sandiego.edu/gen/recording/notes.html#digital.

Sony's official history gives us an inside view of the tremendous impact they have made on the entire music industry and their confidence in the public's response. "When Nakajima's team first began developing the CD, they had projected that CDs would overtake LPs by 1989 and reach a peak production volume of twice that of the LP. This projection had even been pushed forward two to three years to impress on Sony's management the promising future of CDs."

A Japanese proverb says, "It takes ten years for things to change." (Notice Sony's commitment to a long process, not an event.) Sony's history amplifies this statement by letting us know that "Nakajima and his team expected it to take this long (at least ten years) for the CD to replace the LP. It was a wonderful miscalculation. The music industry was given a new life thanks to the CD. Nakajima was overjoyed." The official history goes on to mention that Nakajima said, "Thank God we developed digital technology."

What will the future hold for the music industry? I do not know, except that digital technology has changed all the rules. Today we can't even think about the advancement of technology without including digital technology as a part of the equation. What lessons can we learn from the way Sony created the legendary market "pull" that all of us have experienced over the past decades? How can we apply the push/pull concept to our own enterprises? Marketing guru Terry L. Brock gives us some excellent real-world advice on his blog, with the following six points:

---

1. *Study the Market.*

This is the tough part. We have to be objective like white-coat-wearing scientists who don't care about their own personal feelings but check what the market is saying. Think of yourself as a doctor who is examining a patient for what is wrong. Your own personal feelings and ideas are nice, but what really matters is what the objective, reality-based results say. Find what the market has and needs. Look for gaping holes. Fred Smith saw a big hole in the market for overnight delivery—and then came up with the idea of Federal Express (now FedEx Kinkos). Tom Monaghan, the founder of Dominoes Pizza saw a need for quick, fast delivery of pizzas. Find that need out there.

2. *Use Technology to Investigate.*

Today we have the Internet to help with research. Use tools like WordTracker (www.wordtracker.com) and Google's new Hot Trends (www.google.com/trends/hottrends) to find what a lot of people are interested in right now. This way you're not just relying on your own feelings and opinions. Find what others are saying. This is also a great way for parents to know about "what's hot" with their teens. Visiting Hot Trends is a good way for busy people to stay up-to-date.

3. *Do Your Own Primary Research.*

Find out what real people are saying. Conduct a non-scientific random sampling of your own customers. You can also survey others (www.surveymonkey.com—good tool here) as a way to find answers to common questions.

4. *Do the "Flag Pole" Test.*

This is one of the best I've found. The old phrase of "raise it up the flag pole and see if anyone salutes" works in the real world. Try several ideas. Carefully track which ideas sell. The old marketer's credo of "test, test, and re-test" works here. Successful marketers never stop testing. I remember in market research classes in business school they told us the importance of "testing in Peoria" to find good products. People can say they want Blue Widgets in your surveys. However, if they buy Red Widgets in the store in Peoria with real dollars, that is what the successful marketer notes for reference. Put on your white coat, market researcher, and be objective. Measure. Test.

DAY

1

Name three things that depress or discourage you.
Why? How do these things affect your life?

DAY

2

List two ideas that excite and motivate you. Why?
How much energy have you put into these ideas?

DAY

3

What is the happiest time you can remember in
your life? How has this time informed the way you
currently live your life?

DAY

4

If you were required to become another living person, who might it be? Why this person?

DAY

5

In your opinion, what is the difference between quality time and quantity of time in your relationships? Who are the people in your life who get the quantity of your time?

Evaluate. Yes, it's hard work and would be easier to set back and speculate on what you "think" the market wants. However, your bottom line will be better having implemented scientific testing and measurement.

5. *Gain Quantum Competence.*

You have to be really, really good at what you offer. Don't just give a book report. Get the training, education, and credentials necessary. Develop the products that are sound. You have to have a great product, not just great ideas. Continually upgrade and test your skills and product knowledge. Without a sound product, all the market research you do is just theory.

6. *Don't Throw Away Those Gut Instincts.*

Malcolm Gladwell's book *Blink* tells us about how we judge what is going to work. Sometimes we can have that "gut instinct" but it usually is successful only after lots of real-world experience. Keep testing and trying new ideas. Some don't work. In fact, most of our initial ideas won't work. However, keep working and massaging them, coupled with real-world testing, and you improve your odds on getting what the market wants.

"These steps can help you get more business. It is not easy. . . . But, if you're willing to pay the price, put in the hard thinking work, and do the testing, you'll find what the market wants."

Six Marketing "Pull" Points. © 2007 by Terry L. Brock. Used by permission. View his video and read his blog on this and other topics—yoursuccess.blogspot.com/2007/08/how-to-get-business-push-vs-pull.html.

May you have fun experiencing the "pull" of the marketplace!

Discussion Questions from Chapter Six in the Book and More:

1. Respond to the question, "What do you do?" Write a thirty-second introduction to you and your business—kind of like an "elevator speech." Give the response to another person or in front of a group, and ask for honest feedback:

   - On a scale of one to ten (ten being highest), how compelling is your thirty-second introduction? Rate it yourself, and then ask others to rate it, with comments on how you can improve it.

   - Where does it rank on the "it-sounds-canned" meter?

   - What is the main message you are sending or trying to send?

2. Recently, I was consulting with an upscale art dealer who was frustrated by many of his customers wanting to purchase only the more popular pieces of art. He told me that these particular clients were lazy and didn't want to learn about the subtleties and nuances of some of the lesser-known pieces of beautiful art he had for sale. After listening to him talk for quite a while, I realized that his love for teaching was turning off some of his best clients. I gave him a quick overview of the realities of market "push" and market "pull" and then suggested, "Perhaps you need to categorize which pieces in your gallery are in the 'push' category and which are in the 'pull' category. I can help you develop a quick, user-friendly *Art Acquisition Personality Profile* (AAPP) instrument that helps you understand which clients want to learn more about the philosophy behind certain pieces and which clients really do not want you to teach them but only want to purchase what they like at first glance. Develop separate 'push' and 'pull' rooms in your gallery so that you can take clients to the rooms that fit their art acquisition personality." His eyes brightened with understanding. This concept has literally transformed his customer-service approach to selling art.

   Hitchhiking off this illustration, determine which aspects of your business enterprise require a "push." In which aspects do you experience the market "pull"? Make a list of the two categories, and then determine the marketing strategy around each aspect. Which aspects may require an initial "push" before they can potentially generate the market "pull"? How do you know this?

3. You have probably heard that everyone is tuned into WIIFM: *What's in It for Me?* What do you offer that helps potential customers tune into you, your goods, and your services? What are the felt-need benefits? You already know what's in it for you. What's in it for them? Make a list, and then determine how your marketing plan connects with everything on that list.

4. Make a list of all the spinoff products that you can produce and/or services you can perform.

5. Develop a timeline, and then start creating these projects, one by one until you have exhausted every possible means of leveraging what you have.

6. What kind of time will you commit every day to your vision?

7. How will you reward yourself when you reach certain predetermined goals? Fill in the blanks: "When I reach _____, I will _____." If it is possible, involve your family in the celebration and reward.

8. How does the use of the fax and email fit into your marketing plans?

9. Check out the e-zine concept. Think about having a spot on your website for people to give you their email addresses so that you can send them a periodic email loaded with helpful information. Once permission is given, you can keep on the radar screens of potentially thousands of people who may eventually open other doors of opportunity for you. Make sure that 97.5 percent of what you send is helpful. Don't make it one big advertisement for your business. People will cancel their subscriptions, and your reputation will be toast.

THOUGHTS ON FINANCES AND THE BIBLE FROM A CERTIFIED FINANCIAL PLANNER™:

Check *Week Seven* in the appendix.

Prayer: "Lord, I realize that I am human, with all of the ups and downs of the human experience. I also realize that you created me with the passions, desires, and drives within me. You understand me and know me better than I could ever understand or know myself. Please show me how to channel those passions and drives within, in such a way that I give others a clear view of you, not of me. I want to be excellent in everything I do because I know that this is one of the things that puts a big fat smile on your face. I want to reflect your plans for me, not my own, because I know that your plans for me are much bigger than I could ever dare to dream."

ENHANCING YOUR INFLUENCE

Ancient Wisdom

Proverbs 10:4–5: "Lazy hands make a man poor, but diligent hands bring wealth. He who gathers crops in summer is a wise son, but he who sleeps during harvest is a disgraceful son."

Proverbs 13:18: "He who ignores discipline comes to poverty and shame, but whoever heeds correction is honored."

Proverbs 27:2: "Let another praise you, and not your own mouth."

Reflections

As you read chapter seven in the book, what were your initial thoughts and feelings about what you were reading (positive and/or negative)?

If you were able to communicate with the author while reading this chapter, what would you have said?

What were some thoughts (if any) you had about connecting the contents of this particular chapter to your business enterprise?

Additional Perspectives

The Bible (the manufacturer's handbook) is the most intriguing document, written over a period of about sixteen hundred years, by about forty different writers. The Bible contains history, law, poetry, prophecy, prayers, praises, wisdom, and important instructions for success and living. It was written in a number of different countries, such as Israel, Babylon (now Iraq), Persia (now Iran), Italy (now Italy), and Greece.

Take a look at the table below. The writers were of many different occupations: shepherd (Amos), military leader (Joshua), king/priest (Samuel), farmer (Job), tax collector (Matthew), fisherman (Peter), tent maker (Paul), physician (Luke), prophet (Malachi), and apostle (Paul). None of them were professional writers or religious fanatics.

What a miracle! Try to imagine how it was for that many people, in that many countries, from that many occupations, over that long period of time, writing a book, without previous planning or without being able to consult with each other, that is not contradictory. Only God could be the real author behind such writers.

None of us can or will ever write anything on par with Scripture, but the point is that God used ordinary people to write an extraordinarily unique book. One can only imagine the excuses and rationalizations of some of the more uneducated authors stated to God prior to writing: "Who? Me? You've got to be kidding! Sorry, you got the wrong person on the line!" I would have loved to have been a fly on the wall in the midst of some of those conversations.

Here's a quick overview of some of the writers of the Bible:

PERSON	CLAIM TO FAME	BOOK(S) AUTHORED
Moses	Egyptian prince later charged with treason and exiled	Genesis, Exodus, Leviticus, Numbers, Deuteronomy
Joshua	Israel's Military commander	Most of Joshua
Ruth	Moabitess Gentile, widow, housewife	
Samuel	Priest	Judges and Ruth?
???		I & II Samuel I & II Kings I & II Chronicles
Ezra	priest, scribe, member of "The Great Synagogue"?	Ezra
Nehemiah	Persian king's "press secretary," member of "The Great Synagogue"?	Nehemiah
Esther	queen of the Persian Empire	
Job	rich farmer	
David	Israel's most famous king	About half of the Psalms
Solomon	son of David, Israel's third king	Proverbs, Ecclesiastes, Song of Solomon
Isaiah	prophet, prominent Israeli statesman	Isaiah
Jeremiah	prophet, priestly heritage	Jeremiah, Lamentations
Ezekiel	prophet, priestly heritage	Ezekiel
Daniel	prophet, Babylonian prime minister	Daniel
Hosea	prophet	Hosea
Joel	prophet	Joel
Amos	prophet, uneducated poor shepherd	Amos
Obadiah	prophet	Obadiah
Jonah	prophet, statesman	Jonah
Micah	prophet, poor preacher	Micah
Nahum	prophet	Nahum
Habakkuk	prophet	Habakkuk
Zephaniah	prophet	Zephaniah
Haggai	prophet	Haggai
Zechariah	prophet, priestly heritage, member of "The Great Synagogue"?	Zechariah
Malachi	prophet	Malachi

DAY
1

What can you do well with the least effort, and what can you do well with the most effort? How do you know?

DAY
2

The way you manage money can make the difference, over time, between being able to retire earlier or being able to launch into a new business venture. How well do you budget your money and then follow your budget? How often do you monitor "leaking cash" (unnecessary service fees, banking fees, credit card fees/interest, and carrying debt, paying minimum monthly fees—the "cash drains" that add up over time)?

DAY 3

What can you probably never do well? How comfortable are you with this knowledge?

DAY 4

Can you think of any life lessons you have avoided learning? List them. How important is it for you to learn these particular life lessons?

DAY 5

When did you last take at least thirty minutes to take your bearings and to check your direction? What did you learn about yourself?

PERSON	CLAIM TO FAME	BOOK(S) AUTHORED
Matthew	despised tax collector	Gospel of Matthew
Mark	Peter's scribe and associate	
Luke	Gentile medical doctor, Paul's associate	Gospel of Luke, Acts
John	son of a wealthy, prominent fisherman	Gospel of John, I & II & III John, Revelation
Paul	Pharisee, student of Gamaliel, tentmaker.	Letters to Romans, Corinthians, Galatians, Ephesians, Philippians, Colossians, Thessalonians, Timothy, Titus, Philemon
Timothy	disciple of Paul	
Titus	Gentile fellow worker with Paul	
Philemon	fellow worker with Paul	
Paul???		Hebrews
James	half brother of Jesus	
Peter	fisherman	
Jude	half brother of Jesus	

Let's flip the channel to the here and now. Some people start by writing a brief overview (150 words) of how they got saved and the subsequent change in their lives. It can be produced in an inexpensive folded-tract format—printing thousands (with minimal financial investment) that can be given to people with whom you interact while living your everyday life. This is a very personal way to get the writing juices flowing in your heart and mind. Is this something you are willing to try? If so, when will you have completed it?

Make a list of some topics that interest you. Which topic is the one that would be the best candidate for a book or a booklet? In what areas are you an expert? What questions do people ask the most when around you? What about the history of your business enterprise with your experiences and perspectives plowed into the manuscript? You might be amazed by the amount of information out there that would be intriguing to your potential clients. This could be a way of distinguishing you from all others in your industry. Is this booklet or book something you are willing to do? If so, when will you have completed it?

Discussion Questions from Chapter Seven in the Book and More:

Here are questions you have to ask yourself:

1. What is the purpose of your book? When trying to explain why you are writing a book, remind yourself that it's not about you. It's about the reader.

2. What makes your book different from all others on the same topic?

3. Who is your target audience for the book, and why should they even be interested in what you have to say? Why have you chosen them as your primary readership?

4. How would you describe your writing style?

5. What are some of the ways you can leverage and utilize the booklet you will write? What part does the Internet play in your marketing strategy?

6. How can you help promote it? Am I willing to go on the "rubber chicken" circuit? (Most events you will speak at will serve chicken.)

7. Why would anyone want to read a book written by you? In other words, what gives you the credibility to write about a chosen subject?

8. What goods and services can you develop around your writing project? Make a wish list, with a budget and timeline for each, and then prioritize. Here are a few suggestions to get you started: seminars, audio book edition, workbook, calendars, all-occasion cards, T-shirts, baseball caps, special updated reports, video game, and/or board game, etc.

9. What do you know about developing publicity around your book/ booklet project BEFORE you even start writing it? Make a list of ideas

that can be implemented on a limited budget and another list that can be implemented on a larger budget.

THOUGHTS ON FINANCES AND THE BIBLE FROM A CERTIFIED FINANCIAL PLANNER™:

Check *Week Eight* in the appendix.

Prayer: "Lord, your Word states that I have been fearfully and wonderfully made. Please forgive me for the times I have taken the blessings you have given me for granted. You have given me the resources, the gifts, and the talents for my success. I do not want to abuse or squander what you have given me. Help me live my life to the fullest and then some. Without faith it is impossible to please you. Show me what that means in my life. I want to embark upon enterprises that are impossible without your help."

REINVENTING YOURSELF

Ancient Wisdom

Proverbs 11:15: "He who puts up security for another will surely suffer, but whoever refuses to strike hands in pledge is safe."

Proverbs 12:18: "Reckless words pierce like a sword, but the tongue of the wise brings healing."

Proverbs 14:15: "A simple man believes anything, but a prudent man gives thoughts to his steps."

Proverbs 16:18: "Pride goes before destruction, a haughty spirit before a fall."

Reflections

As you read chapter eight in the book, what were your initial thoughts and feelings about what you were reading (positive and/or negative)?

If you were able to communicate with the author while reading this chapter, what would you have said?

What were some thoughts (if any) you had about connecting the contents of this particular chapter to your business enterprise?

Additional Perspectives

Reinvention. A word that strikes terror in the hearts of some and stirs up a sense of excitement in others. To everyone it is the hinge upon which the door of opportunity turns.

Adaptability and flexibility are important components of the reinvention process. There are many examples of biblical characters who were forced to reinvent themselves. What forced this change? It was different in each case.

Having grown up in a small fishing village on the shores of the Sea of Galilee, Peter had zero experience outside the very tiny geographical and cultural region surrounding his home in Capernaum. Peter was the heir apparent to his father's fishing business. What other options were available to such an uneducated country bumpkin?

Then Peter looked into the eyes of One who would change the course of his life. He heard a gentle but firm command: "Leave your nets, Peter, and I will make you a fisher of men." For some reason he obeyed, leaving the fishing industry that he had known all his life. No guarantees of financial success. No contract. No promises, except that it was going to be a tough, uncertain road ahead.

What a change! There was very little in Peter's prior life that could prepare him for preaching in front of thousands at Pentecost, walking on water, becoming a highly respected church leader, or ultimately being crucified upside down—immortalized forever as a martyr for the faith.

Jonah became a preacher to the hated Ninevites. It was a long journey from being the patriotic architect of the Israeli coastline to watching thousands of citizens of Nineveh repent. (See 2 Kings 14:25 and Jonah 1:1–4:11.) With every fiber of his being he tried to avoid the new assignment, ending up in the belly of a huge fish for three days.

Ruth left the bad memories and famine of Moab, traveling to an uncertain future in Israel. While gleaning the leftovers of a harvested wheat field, she met the man of her dreams. She had to reinvent herself, from being defined as a poor widow from a foreign nation to being identified as the wife of Boaz, a man of great prominence, and the mother of a son who brought history one generation closer to the birth of the Messiah. (See Ruth 4:13–22.)

David, a shepherd, had to become a warrior when he heard about Goliath. This event, along with being anointed by the prophet Samuel, changed his destiny. He became a mighty king, ruling for forty years.

But these are not the only biblical examples of reinvention. What about Joseph having a dream, being sold as a slave, and ultimately becoming the grand vizier of Egypt? Did Mary and Joseph have any specific training on how to raise the Messiah? Did Noah have a boat-building degree from the local community college?

Someone sent me an email with the following title: *"Everything I need to know, I learned from Noah's Ark."* I have no idea as to who wrote this and will include that information in future editions if the identity of the author is discovered. Here are the wisdom lessons:

1. Don't miss the boat.
2. Remember, we are all in the same boat.
3. Plan ahead. It wasn't raining when Noah built the ark.
4. Stay fit. When you are sixty years old, someone may ask you to do something big.
5. Don't listen to critics; just get on with the job that needs to be done.
6. Build your future on high ground.
7. For safety's sake, travel in pairs.
8. Speed isn't always an advantage. The snails were on board with the cheetahs.
9. When you are stressed, float awhile.

10. Remember, the ark was built by amateurs; the *Titanic* by professionals.
11. No matter the storm, when you are with God, there's always a rainbow waiting.

Very thought provoking. If you have ever had the reinvention process thrust upon you, you are in good company. Like Noah, literally billions of people—since the dawn of time—have been challenged by change. In the biblical framework, there are a number of experiences that can change one's direction: a famine, the threat of war, getting knocked off a horse, a dream, a word of wisdom from a more experienced person, or a chance encounter with Jesus.

How flexible are you? How do you approach change? Give a recent example (good or bad) on how you dealt with change. On a scale of one to ten (ten being "very flexible"), how flexible are you when life brings situations that can bend you to the ground?

Is flexibility always good? Are there some times when it is good to fight back and refuse to bend?

Professional life coach Melanie Keveles suggests ten principles for you to ponder as you consider how you might reinvent your work and your life (used by permission, OnlineCoaching.com):

1. **Stay open and flexible.** Keep your options open and go with the flow. Don't turn down opportunities just because they are outside of the parameters of what you have thought to be your job title or place in life.

2. **Cross pollinate.** Take your ideas, skills and know-how from one field to another. Step outside your comfort zone. Look for ideas from others to bring into your field. Plant your ideas within entirely new fields.

3. **Follow your heart's desire.** Your heart is a wise barometer of what you need to be doing with your life. Don't overrule it entirely with practical suggestions from other people or with notions your mind invents.

4. **Live a little—life experience provides hints.** The more experiences you accumulate, the more you get a view of what works for you and what doesn't. These experiences provide the fodder for continuous

reinventions of yourself. Through these experiences you amass wisdom and skills that will become invaluable to you in your next pursuits.

5. **Visualize**. Paint a picture in your mind's eye of what you want in your life. See this image occurring as you fall asleep at night and upon awakening in the morning. Take every chance to experience this inner image with all of your five senses.

6. **Be curious.** Keep your eyes and ears open and your antenna up for new people and new ideas to enter your life.

7. **Network like crazy.** Make a point to meet new people as often as you can. New people in your life will enrich you and lead you to new opportunities.

8. **Overcome the "know-it-all" stages of life.** Adopt a beginner's mind. Even if you are well schooled, you have much more to learn.

9. **Be a lifelong learner.** Seek new ways to stretch yourself. Find new challenges to master. Attend classes, workshops, read numerous books.

10. **Embrace new ideas and technology.** Don't get locked in a time warp, only interested in the gadgets and gizmos you knew when you were young.

Here are some suggestions for what you can do as you embrace these principles:

- Take on a principle each week. If you agree with a principle— why? If you disagree—why?

- Each morning, journal about how staying more open and flexible than you usually are could affect your life. Or journal about any of the other principles.

- Find a new pursuit that allows you to approach it as a beginner.

- Consider what your work life would look like to someone from Ireland. Or Bolivia. Or Mars.

- Add to this list your own reinventing-yourself principles, such as pray about things that bother you, and study the Bible for verses that apply to your situation.

DAY
1

What is your strongest point as a person? How do you know and when did you discover this?

DAY
2

What is your weakest point as a person? How do you know and when did you discover this?

DAY
3

How are you unlike most people you know? How did this awareness come about?

DAY

4

Give an example of intuition in your life. If possible, list two ways this has helped you avoid trouble.

DAY

5

For important activities that need more priority, where do you find the additional time?

Discussion Questions from Chapter Eight in the Book and More:

1. What forced biblical characters to reinvent themselves?

2. In what way did the bad situations prepare them for future greatness?

3. How many income streams can you produce in your field of interest, without losing your focus?

4. Take a look back on your life. Make a list of the times you've had to reinvent yourself. Celebrate each reinvention, and then glean the wisdom lessons from each.

5. What is the entrepreneurial passion(s) you have considered for many years and maybe even longed to do, but never acted on it?

6. What needs to occur to integrate that particular passion into your life as you are currently experiencing it?

7. What are the top three priorities in your life at this time?

8. Are you living your life in harmony with these priorities? If so, how have these priorities informed the direction of your life at this time? If not, what needs to change so that you are in sync with what you value?

9. Is there an aspect of that entrepreneurial passion that can be brought forward and into your life now and in the future months?

10. At times, life can seem to be like agitated mud in a stirred-up pond. Permitting the mud to settle, with the water clearing up, is something that takes time. Make a list of the unsettled, stirred-up stuff (including your fears) in your life right now, along with the anticipated amount of time for each item to clear up.

11. If you are considering a drastic reinvention of yourself (like going back to school or changing careers), how many incremental steps can you list—moving from where you are right now to where you want to be? Attach a timeline to that list.

12. Do a full 360-degree view around your reinvention potential by making a list of ways you can understand all of the aspects of this personal change. In the list include items like participating in online discussion boards, visiting your local library, reading a few books/biographies on the topic, networking with people who are already in the field you want to enter or have made their own life-altering moves—with some personal wisdom to share, etc.

13. Let go of the old and embrace the reinvention process—the new. You will flourish. There are many who have gone on before us . . .

THOUGHTS ON FINANCES AND THE BIBLE FROM A CERTIFIED FINANCIAL PLANNER™:
Check *Week Nine* in the appendix.

Prayer: "Lord, I know that you are the God of second chances. Reinvention is what you are all about! There are times that I get so works oriented that I cannot seem to comprehend how your grace and mercy could be showered on to me. I have heard that when I am the weakest, I become the wonderful target of your grace. Your grace can be given to me only when I deserve it the least. This is hard for me, a recovering workaholic, to grasp. Everything I have ever done, I have earned through my own hard work. You applaud my good works and faith, but I am beginning to realize that the only reason I can ever possess the boldness to walk into your presence is not because of my efforts; it is because of the sacrifice that was made for me on Calvary.

You allowed your blood to be spilled so that I could have access into your presence. May I never, never forget this fact."

SO, WHAT'S YOUR FEE?

Ancient Wisdom

Proverbs 9:10–11: "The fear of the LORD is the beginning of wisdom, and knowledge of the Holy One is understanding. For through me your days will be many, and years will be added to your life."

Proverbs 16:8: "Better a little with righteousness than much gain with injustice."

Proverbs 22:9: "A generous man will himself be blessed."

Proverbs 28:22: "A stingy man is eager to get rich."

Reflections

As you read chapter nine in the book, what were your initial thoughts and feelings about what you were reading (positive and/or negative)?

If you were able to communicate with the author while reading this chapter, what would you have said?

What were some thoughts (if any) you had about connecting the contents of this particular chapter to your business enterprise?

Additional Perspectives

Matthew 25:14–30. The parable of the talents is one of the main stories Jesus told to help us understand the value of time and money. Take a moment to read the parable in your Bible.

In order to understand the meaning and the application of the parable of the talents, we must take note of the crucial terms and their meanings. Let me call your attention to the most important elements of the parable, as I now understand it. Bob Deffinbaugh discusses two elements that are important to understand.

The element of time. Time has been a significant factor in our Lord's teaching concerning his coming and the end of the age, beginning in Matthew 24. (Author's note: I realize that the eschatological views of different churches vary. If your "end time/prophetic" interpretations differ from Mr. Deffinbaugh's, please do not make it an issue in this discussion. It'll all pan out in the end. Simply smile and then move on to the next point.) Jesus made it clear that his return would not be immediate, but after much trouble and the passing of a considerable period of time. While there would be sufficient evidence for his followers to discern the general "season" of his return, neither the day nor the hour would be known (Matthew 24:32–36, 42). Beyond this, his return would come at a time when it was not expected (Matthew 24:44). In the parable of the talents, there are two clear references to time. First, the master stayed away for a long time (Matthew 25:19). Second, the faithful servants immediately went to work to increase their master's money (Matthew 25:16–17).

The element of money. It is, indeed, unfortunate that the term "talent" means something very different today from what our Lord meant when he told this parable. The talent was the largest measurement of money in those days. Since a talent was actually a measurement of weight, it did not have a constant value. A talent of gold, for example, would be worth a whole lot more than a talent of bronze. While commentators differ somewhat over the approximate value of a talent in today's economy, all would agree that it was a large amount of money. Some say that it was the equivalent to twenty years' wages for a common laborer. We must remember, then, that a talent is a measure of money; it is not a reference to abilities. The talents were distributed on the basis of ability, not as the bestowing of ability.

In *The Bible Exposition Commentary* Warren Wiersbe writes, "The talents represent opportunities to use our abilities. If five talents were given to a person with minimal ability, he would be destroyed by the heavy responsibility. But if one talent were given to a man of great ability, he would be disgraced and degraded. God assigns work and opportunity according to ability. We are living in a period of time between Matthew 25:18 and 19. We have been assigned our ministries according to the abilities and gifts God has given us. It is our privilege to serve the Lord and multiply His goods."

God has given all of us at least one talent. Can you identify the talent(s) God has given you? If you have a problem responding to that question, ask someone else to give you an objective perspective.

God has given us the same amount of time. No one gets more and no one gets less. How are you doing with the management of your time? How can you be a better manager of your time?

DAY

1

What is the best piece of "luck" you have ever had? What are the connectors, if any, with that piece of "luck" and any of your past successes or failures?

DAY

2

What is your greatest fear? How do you know this is your greatest fear, and when does it affect your life? In what ways?

DAY
3

When are you most likely to react with anger?
How do others know when you are angry, and
how do they react? What are the assets and
liabilities of expressing your anger? Make a list of
both items.

DAY
4

What kind of work is play for you? When was the
last time you experienced this?

DAY
5

How do you view the passage of time? Do you
fight it or welcome it?

Discussion Questions from Chapter Nine in the Book and More:

1. In view of the elements of time and money, what is your time worth?

2. How do you use time to sharpen and invest your talent(s) as an entrepreneur?

3. Do you know of anyone who could become your agent? What will your approach be, and how will you make it worth his or her time and energy?

4. How comfortable are you talking about the money side of things, on a scale of one to ten, with one being "very comfortable" and ten "extremely uncomfortable." Who generally raises the issue of the fee, you or the potential client? I suggest that you follow your intuition regarding this aspect of the discussion of your fees.

5. What fees do you currently charge? Why? What do you want to charge? Why? How and when will you raise your fees to that higher level?

6. On a separate sheet of paper, draw a line down the center. On one half, list the upside of raising your fees, and on the other half, list the downside of raising your fees. Make a decision and closely monitor the results. The law of diminishing returns is no respecter of person. When the economy starts falling, interest in anything in the service industry falls with it, regardless of how talented or well known you are.

THOUGHTS ON FINANCES AND THE BIBLE FROM A CERTIFIED FINANCIAL PLANNER™:

Check *Week Ten* in the appendix.

Prayer: "Lord, it is you who has given me whatever talents I possess. You also have given me a time to utilize those talents to pay for my weekly and monthly bills. Please show me how to use my time and talents for your honor and glory. Help me to turn my bill-paying sessions into times of thanksgiving and praise for your kindness toward me and my household."

WORK HARD, WORK SMART

Ancient Wisdom

Proverbs 12:15: 'The way of a fool seems right to him, but a wise man listens to advice."

Proverbs 12:16: "A fool shows annoyance at once, but a prudent man overlooks an insult."

Proverbs 13:10: "Pride only breeds quarrels, but wisdom is found in those who take advice."

Proverbs 13:22: "A good man leaves an inheritance for his children's children."

Reflections

As you read chapter ten in the book, what were your initial thoughts and feelings about what you were reading (positive and/or negative)?

If you were able to communicate with the author while reading this chapter, what would you have said?

What were some thoughts (if any) you had about connecting the contents of this particular chapter to your business enterprise?

Additional Perspectives

Jesus said that he was going to build a church against which the gates of hell would not prevail. This was an insurmountable task, especially since his public ministry lasted about three years. If you were Jesus' chief of staff, what would have been your advice, knowing that he would have short time to accomplish such an enormous task?

In that position, I probably would have encouraged him to adopt at least three public relations strategies:

1. He definitely needed to pick better, more qualified disciples.
2. When he spoke to the multitudes, I probably would have asked him to consider using angels, special effects when illustrating certain points, and levitating himself about twelve feet above the crowd. Any onlooker would've been convinced that Jesus was an extremely important person—one worth following.
3. Knowing that he had the power to disappear and then to appear in another geographical location, I would have encouraged him to do breakfast with the Nazareth town fathers at 8:00 AM, schedule an appearance in Capernaum at 10:00 AM, be in Jerusalem for lunch with important business executives, and then Beersheba at 2:00 PM, Athens

at 3:00 PM, Corinth at 4:00 PM, Ephesus for supper, and an evening seminar event in Rome. His daily schedule would be grueling, and only certain influential people would get access to him. The next day would be more of the same.

With the benefits of twenty-twenty hindsight, we know that everything worked out perfectly and that I would have messed things up if I were the one in charge of his time and the development of his marketing strategy.

It has been said that the *good* is the enemy of the *best*. To illustrate this concept, Charles E. Hummel wrote a small but powerful booklet in 1967 entitled *Tyranny of the Urgent*. I read it at least once a year to clarify my focus in life. It has changed my life by helping me identify the *urgent* things I permit in my schedule, which tend to crowd out the *important*.

Hummel states, "In the great prayer of John 17 Jesus said, 'I have finished the work which thou gavest me to do.' How could Jesus use the word *finished*? His three-year ministry seemed all too short. . . .Yet on that last night, with many useful tasks undone and urgent human needs unmet, the Lord had peace; he knew he had finished God's work. The Gospel records show that Jesus worked hard. . . . Yet his life was never feverish. He had time for people. He could spend hours talking to one person, such as the Samaritan woman at the well. His life showed a wonderful sense of balance, a sense of timing."

This is intriguing to me. A day later Jesus was on the cross, uttering the words, "It is finished." How could he say this when at that specific moment there were still rampant needs all over the known world? Lepers, blind people, and the lame were still in need of healing. Marriages were in need of reconciliation. Demon-possessed people were in need of deliverance. Orphans were in need of food and shelter. Unemployed people everywhere were in need of jobs.

With all of the special powers and means of travel available to him, we never read of Jesus running from one place to another, galloping on a horse, or traveling in a chariot. The only time he uses an alternative means of travel is when we read of him riding a donkey into Jerusalem.

Hummel goes on to ask, "What was the secret of Jesus' work? We find a clue following Mark's account of Jesus' busy day in Mark 1:35. Here is the secret of Jesus' life and work for God: He prayerfully waited for his Father's instructions and for the strength to follow them. Jesus had no divinely-drawn

DAY

1

If you could live for another one hundred years, what would you do with the time allotted? If you believe in an afterlife, how does that knowledge affect your present decisions and priorities?

DAY

2

Is there unforgiveness or bitterness you harbor toward anyone? If so, in what ways has it controlled or altered your life? What can you do, if anything, to resolve this?

DAY
3

What part of your life would you like to change or relive? Why?

DAY
4

Beyond career or material success, what is the core purpose of your life? How would anyone else know?

DAY
5

List the tasks you really enjoy. What sense of fulfillment do you feel from doing these tasks?

blueprint; he discerned the Father's will day by day in a life of prayer. By this means he warded off the urgent and accomplished the important."

Prayer and meditation on the Word of God seem to be the best ways to live our lives in accordance with his. What is the assignment God has given you? Has he given you more than one? In what ways are you avoiding the distractions of busyness to fulfill what he has given you to do?

Every night when your head hits the pillow you can say, "I still have many things on my list that need to be accomplished, but I finished my work for today. I did the best I could with the time and opportunities allotted me. Tomorrow is another day. Lord, if you do choose to give me breath tomorrow, I look forward to spending time with you, so that you can help me accomplish all that you have for me to accomplish for your kingdom."

In what ways did the following biblical characters work hard and smart?

> **Moses**. Clue: Delegation will increase your influence and will help you with time management. Read Exodus 18 (entire chapter) for more insight.

> **Nehemiah**. Clue: Be willing to do the unglamorous work and research when everyone else is asleep. Read Nehemiah 2:11–16 for more insight.

> **Ezra**. Clue: God's favor will open doors of opportunity that money cannot purchase and power cannot influence. Read 2 Chronicles 36:21–23 and Ezra 1 (entire chapter) for more insight.

Discussion Questions from Chapter Ten in the Book and More:

1. What factors would motivate you to want to offer your services for less than you would normally charge? Write the factors down on a separate sheet of piece of paper, and reflect on them the next time you are asked to do a freebie.

2. Do not be motivated by financial desperation for a gig, guilt, or your need to be needed the next time someone asks you to do a freebie. What would motivate you to step out of what you would normally do

for a person or what you would normally charge for your services?

3. What kind of boundaries do you set for yourself? Are those boundaries realistic when compared to the vision you desire to fulfill?

4. Is the vision you desire to fulfill realistic when compared to the boundaries you have set for yourself?

5. Have you heard this story? Two shoe salesmen travel to a small developing nation in search of new business opportunities. One man calls his wife the moment he lands, telling her, "Honey, I'm coming back home. There's no hope here. Nobody here is wearing shoes, so there's no one to sell to." He boards the next flight home. The second man calls his wife and says, "Honey, you wouldn't believe what I found here. There is so much opportunity. No one here is wearing shoes. I can sell to the whole country!"

   A pessimist will focus on at least ONE problem in the middle of all the available opportunities. An optimist will focus on at least ONE opportunity in the middle of all the problems. Paul Harvey said it right: "*I have never seen a monument erected to a pessimist.*" List the wisdom lessons you can glean from the shoe-salesmen illustration. What are the overuses of pessimists and optimists? Discuss how to apply all of this information in your business.

   - "*Apparent open opportunities—Closed minds.*"
     Discuss this concept, with personal illustrations.

   - "*Apparent closed opportunities—Open minds.*"
     Discuss this concept, with personal illustrations.

6. Share the last time you absolutely knew that you were working hard and also working smart at the same time. What was happening within you and around you?

THOUGHTS ON FINANCES AND THE BIBLE FROM A CERTIFIED FINANCIAL PLANNER™:

Check *Week Eleven* in the appendix.

Prayer: "Lord, help me understand the power of waiting on you, listening for your guidance in my life. The reality that you want to spend time with me is still a mystery to me, but I rejoice in the fact that your desire to love me is greater than my need to understand. Thank you for the resources you have given me. Without you, I can do nothing. Help me to grasp the significance of that truth."

BARTERING YOUR SERVICES

Ancient Wisdom

Proverbs 6:6–8: "Go to the ant, you sluggard; consider its way and be wise! . . . It stores its provisions in summer and gathers its food in harvest."

Proverbs 12:22: "The LORD detests lying lips, but he delights in men who are truthful."

Proverbs 16:32: "Better a patient man than a warrior, a man who controls his temper than one who takes a city."

Proverbs 22:29: "Do you see a man skilled at his work? He will serve before kings."

Reflections

As you read chapter eleven in the book, what were your initial thoughts and feelings about what you were reading (positive and/or negative)?

If you were able to communicate with the author while reading this chapter, what would you have said?

What were some thoughts (if any) you had about connecting the contents of this particular chapter to your business enterprise?

Additional Perspectives

Moses was in the desert when God told him the following: "Tell the Israelites to bring me an offering. You are to receive the offering for me from each man whose heart prompts him to give. These are the offerings you are to receive from them: gold, silver and bronze; blue, purple and scarlet yarn and fine linen; goat hair; ram skins dyed red and hides of sea cows; acacia wood; olive oil for the light; spices for the anointing oil and for the fragrant incense" (Exodus 25:2–6).

All of this was to be done in preparation for the building of the tabernacle. Not everyone could give silver or gold. Some could give yarn or a ram's hide. Olive oil was the only thing that others could give. Still others could only give manual labor.

God was interested in allowing everyone to participate in the giving of goods and services. As you can see, no one was left out. The poor, the lower class, the middle class, and the wealthy could all participate in the building of the tabernacle in some manner.

Barter has some similar elements to it. If time is money, giving of one's time in a manner that is valuable to another is a worthwhile trade. The barter system has been around since biblical times. It is the exchanging goods or services with each other on an "as needed" basis. For example, a general contractor might build a backyard deck for a mechanic in exchange for having the transmission fixed on his automobile. A simple concept, bartering becomes rather complex when trying to implement exchanges among millions of people!

- Living Animals (cattle, horses, oxen, sheep)
- Animal Parts (skins, leather, ivory, seashells)
- Crops (various grains, spices, tea, sugar)
- Tools (agricultural implements such as spades and hoes)
- Weapons (spears, arrows, knives, swords)
- Minerals (salt)
- Stones (diamonds, rubies, emeralds)
- Metals (gold, silver, copper, bronze, iron, brass, tin, platinum)
- Crafted Objects (beads, garments, wampum)
- Coins (made from various metals)
- Paper (currency, checks)

Bartering is a terribly inefficient and inconvenient system on a larger scale. But on a smaller scale, it can work. Today we use coin and paper. In the future it may be electronic units! It doesn't really matter so long as we all ascribe value to it and universally accept it.

I was intrigued by the real-world issues facing David Gomm, a stained glass designer. I thought that a glimpse into his world might give some insights about the ups and the downs of bartering to the rest of us. The following is an article written by David entitled "Should I Ever Barter Away My Stained Glass Art or Should I Hold Out for Cash?"

> In the past, we've, of course, had many occasions to make cash deals on our stained glass art and occasionally we've had a chance to barter our stained glass art for goods and services. Over the course of years, we've had some barters and trades that worked out well, but many trades seemed to go sour.
>
> Most started out with each party having the best of

intentions to do right by the other, but our experiences were that each time the trade or barter was made, our stained glass went right out at the start of the trade and then we usually got our part of the trade after the fact. As a result, the folks we traded with were always sure of what they were getting, but we never seemed to know exactly what we would get, so we ended up getting disappointed most times.

As we've entered into these non-cash deals, we've developed three simple rules or guidelines to help us avoid the bad deals, while leaving the door open for the good ones.

Rule One: Know What to Trade For

We've learned that if we're not careful, we could end up trading away all the work we could possibly do and leave ourselves with no more materials to make more glass pieces. So this first rule helps us to avoid trading away more than we can afford. As stained glass artists, we know that 10 to 20 percent of the retail price of a window is the cost of the materials that go into the window and the rest of the price reflects the cost of our labor and some profit for the company. So we've adopted the policy that we never trade away the cost of the window. We will make a trade, but not at our own expense. So when we make a deal, we agree that at least 10 or 20 percent of the trade be in cash, to cover the cost of materials. And we put the cash back into the business for the purpose of purchasing replacement goods. This keeps us from losing on the deal, in the event that what we trade for ends up with little or no value to us.

Back when we first started doing windows, we had a friend who wanted a specific design. She drew a sketch of a very nice pattern which was an amalgam of three different designs she had seen. We agreed that the panel would be about a thousand dollars (which was low for the amount of work) and we started building the panel. Now, up to this point, the window was going to be a cash deal, very straightforward, very clean. But once I had half the window cut out, her husband decided to get into the act and turned the deal into a trade. He was very aggressive in his negotiating skills and I was a wimp. He beat me down on price from $1000 to $300. Why I ever agreed to that change still confuses me, but then he took the cash away from the deal and made it a trade for construction parts that he had lying around. The deal went from bad to worse! I was already committed to the window since the glass was cut, so I allowed the deal to go downhill. I ended up spending $300 on solder for the window (solder had temporarily jumped in price), and I got what the husband valued as $300 worth of construction parts. They really were pretty much worthless. But the deal taught me several valuable lessons. The most important was rule one: Know What to Trade For. I had learned to spell out what the trade was to be, how much cash would be involved, and to get a deposit or the entire balance of the cash part of the deal before cutting any glass.

Another instance vividly illustrates what NOT to trade for. We've learned that whenever someone comes to us for classes or to get a stained glass window built and they start whining about cost, or acting "poor mouth" and then they advance the idea of a trade, we ALWAYS lose on the deal.

April was a good example of this type of bad deal. She came and started to take classes. But she immediately began wondering if she could make payments instead of paying for class up-front. We agreed and then the next week, she advanced the idea that maybe she could trade for half of the cost of tuition. We asked what she had in mind and she told us about these beautiful candles she made. So we decided to allow the trade. She traded us two candles which she felt were worth the $40 of class she was trading for. I would have valued them at $10 total, but we'd already entered into the trade and felt committed. So we allowed to let the trade stand. The candles, while overvalued on her part, also had another problem. They stunk! We couldn't be in the same room with them, and we gave them away to someone who didn't find them offensive. That deal started out badly, and we allowed it to continue, not putting an end to it when we began to feel taken advantage of. We've since found that all those type of deals have been bad for us, both in the trade itself and also in the bad feelings it generates in us. It damages our faith and trust in others when we get ripped off. A footnote to this instance, when April quit coming to class, she left owing us almost as much money as she had paid for her classes.

Rule Two: Get Your End First

It's human nature to be quite excited while you're about to get something, but to lose interest once you've gotten your side of the deal. The donkey who follows the carrot on a stick is a good example. As long as that carrot hangs out there nearly within reach, the donkey will keep moving, but as soon as the carrot is gone, the donkey stops. We even lose some of our enthusiasm for completing a project when we've been paid, but we usually have plans and patterns that have been set in advance, so our part of a trade or a business transaction continues on whether there is a promise or a reward.

This isn't the case with folks we've traded with. So we're fighting two negatives if we don't get our part of the trade up front. First we're dealing with something (an item or service) which is sight unseen and we're fighting the other person's natural loss of enthusiasm for the trade because they've already gotten what they wanted.

A good example of a positive barter was when we traded for some essential oil diffusers for Christmas presents with a client. We got about $400 worth of product in trade for some work we did for them. Over the course of the year, we were able to complete their design and get their windows installed for them. Then at Christmas time the next year we traded for some essential oils for the balance of what they owed us. This was a good trade because it allowed us to save on the costs of Christmas presents for two years and it got them a beautiful entryway that will give them years of enjoyment.

A trade which didn't go so well involved a custom rocking chair built by a friend's brother. The trade went fairly smoothly except we didn't like the custom rocking chair once it was completed. It was too high, and didn't rock right. It was beautiful and we gave it to my sister and her husband. They loved it, he was taller and the rock of the chair was just right for him. In this case, the deal went just as it should have, but we were just trading for something sight unseen.

Rule Three: Give More Than Expected, Lower Your Own Expectations

To really get a deal to work in the favor of both parties, you've got to give more than the other guy expects, always trying to make the deal better for them. And you'll be less disappointed when you lower your own expectations. When I dealt with the husband who traded construction parts to me, I learned that many times the other guy doesn't care if you get a good deal. This man was only interested in getting a good deal for himself, and he did. But I never traded stained glass with him again!

A good barter arrangement is one where both parties are concerned with the other's feelings. When we made a trade with an artist friend, some large windows for a painting, the deal changed several times. They agreed to pay for the materials and we would get two paintings, based on the amount of time that it would take to build both of the art projects. She later decided that two paintings were too much so we agreed to get one and some design time on glass projects. When it turned out that the completed painting couldn't be published in the magazine we had thought it would be placed in, we felt that the ultimate value of the painting was greatly diminished. So the deal did continue to go downhill, to become less valuable to us, through no one's fault, just circumstances. But we had already lowered our expectations and our friend had become a greater friend and we have enjoyed many hours doing art projects together.

We have another friend, whom we build pieces for on a fairly regular basis. The trades never go well for us, she forgets that we have credit with her and she wants more glass, we will never get "even" but we've lowered our expectations. We know her, know she "needs" the pieces we trade with her and figure that the work we do for her is more a gift than a trade.

If you can get to this point, where you expect little in a

DAY 1

What does it mean to be a person of wisdom? Are you such a person? How do you know?

DAY 2

Are you content with whom or what you are becoming? By the way, who or what *are* you becoming? How would your best friend respond to the same question about you?

DAY 3

If a casual observer were to observe the way you live your life, what would he or she deduce your definition of success to be? On a scale of one to ten (ten being "extremely satisfied"), how comfortable are you with this definition?

DAY
4

How will you know when you've achieved success
in your life?

DAY
5

How do you know when you are taking a real
time-out? How often does this happen? If it has
not been your habit, do you feel ready to try
it during the next couple of weeks? If so, write
down the time you will set aside and what you
will do or not do.

trade—where it's more about opportunity, art, and building beauty—bartering might work out for you. If you find yourself feeling ripped off, you should probably avoid trading your art and stick to cash deals. Even they will occasionally go south on you.

Trading stained glass for products and services has very often been a way for others to obtain the glass that they want, when they really wouldn't have been able to afford it for cash. It has seldom been a good way for us to fill our bank account, but it has often been a way for us to develop relationships with others who have become dear to us and has become a way for our art to be seen by others. It very often leads to other deals we would never have imagined, providing us with sales in the most unlikely places. It's like that Scripture about casting thy bread upon the waters and it will return to you ten fold. A good trade is like that. It returns to us rewards we never would have imagined.

Used by permission. David Gomm is a stained glass artist and author whose work can be seen at GommStudios.com.

Discussion Questions from Chapter Eleven in the Book and More:

1. What do you agree with or disagree with regarding the bartering information shared by David Gomm about his stained glass business? Why? How has this information informed your own bartering strategies?

2. What goods or services can you leverage into a win-win bartering situation?

3. What has your accountant told you about the potential tax ramifications of bartering?

4. Who in your geographical region would benefit from your goods and services?

5. Who internationally can benefit from your goods or services?

6. How can a win-win situation develop?

7. How will they know about this win-win situation unless you tell them? How can you create the demand for what you have to offer?

8. After doing research, what are the bartering networks in your region, and how can you participate?

9. How can barter be used in debt collection?

10. Many barter relationships eventually develop into real cash business arrangements as the bartering entities grow in trust and mutual respect for one another. How can this win-win strategy work for you?

THOUGHTS ON FINANCES AND THE BIBLE FROM A CERTIFIED FINANCIAL PLANNER™:
Check *Week Twelve* in the appendix.

Prayer: "Lord, help me to always look for ways to help others be successful before I look to make my own success. It is my desire that everyone I work with is benefited by my talents, skills, and friendship. I know that you will take care of my needs in the process. Teach me to have a giving spirit. Teach me how to have wisdom as I share, barter, or give of the talents you have given me."

THE CURIOSITY-DRIVEN LIFE

Ancient Wisdom

Proverbs 13:7: "One man pretends to be rich, yet has nothing; another pretends to be poor, yet has great wealth."

Proverbs 15:19: "The way of the sluggard is blocked with thorns, but the path of the upright is a highway."

Proverbs 16:13: "Kings take pleasure in honest lips; they value a man who speaks the truth."

Reflections

As you read chapter twelve in the book, what were your initial thoughts and feelings about what you were reading (positive and/or negative)?

If you were able to communicate with the author while reading this chapter, what would you have said?

What were some thoughts (if any) you had about connecting the contents of this particular chapter to your business enterprise?

Additional Perspectives

What if just a few of us possessed absolute knowledge that the price of gold was going to double in value a week from next Thursday? How would that change our focus over the next week? Pause and really think about it. I have pondered such fantasies, searching for practical applications to my life. The main thought that emerges is, "The knowledge of future events directly impacts present-day priorities and decisions."

Revelations 1:3 states that we are blessed if we read—and really take to heart—the prophetic words in the Book of Revelation. One blessing that I believe emerges is that we begin to develop clarity about our current priorities. In other words, like anticipating the doubling of the price of gold, the knowledge of eternity (future events) impacts our current decisions.

How does this relate to your entrepreneurial journey? I can respond to that question with a few more questions. What really matters fifty years from now? A thousand years from now? What is the purpose of wealth? What is driving you to be successful in your business? Do you believe that you will be personally standing before the Lord one day? If so, try to imagine that moment as you consider the main purpose of your life in the here and now.

Read Revelation 21 and 22 to gain a fresh vision of heaven. A glorious city 1,500 miles square. Crystal clear walls 216 feet thick. Twelve pearly gates. Streets of transparent gold. Emerald. Amethyst. Jasper. Beryl. Topaz. All tears wiped away. No more sickness, death, curses, grieving, police/fire sirens, or pain. The former things are passed away.

Read the parable of hidden treasure in Matthew 13:44, and try to grasp the essence of that story in the here and now—in light of eternity. In Bible times wealthy people would hide their gold and silver in odd places because there were no secure banks. Sometimes the person who hid the treasure would die suddenly or a roving army would take him and his neighbors captive. The secret about the hidden treasure would be lost with his absence. Generations later, in a new civilization, a poor farm hand could very well have stumbled on to a treasure like this. It is possible that his family thought he was a lunatic to sell everything he owned to buy such a field—until they saw the treasure. "The kingdom of heaven is like treasure hidden in a field. When a man found it, he hid it again, and then in his joy went and sold all he had and bought that field."

How does this apply to you and to me? What is the treasure you have found? How did you find it? What is the field you have "purchased" because of that treasure? What did you "sell" to purchase that field? What are you doing in your life that requires that kind of sacrifice? Who thought you were crazy to "purchase such a field" apparently filled with rocks, bramble bushes, and briar patches?

In our kitchen we have a statement stuck on our refrigerator, "Live in a way that makes absolutely no sense unless there is a life to come."

168-Hour Week

We're all for the afterlife, but what are we supposed to do in the meantime? In the middle of too much, too fast, how are we supposed to take time for God?

Every day you live is another day you won't get back. Everyone who has ever lived has the same amount of hours in a day. Rich or poor, famous or not—it's the same resource for everyone. This fact of life on earth is the great equalizer. Why is it that some people accomplish so much more than others? Perhaps it is because of the choices made about how to fulfill our individual purpose in the time allotted each of us.

DAY

1

Is there anything you want to change about your criteria for success and what it is you are striving for? What will you do about this? When?

DAY

2

What do you believe about people in general? How does your behavior reveal this general belief about people?

DAY

3

What gives you hope for the future when things seem to go wrong in your work, your relationships, or in the world at large?

DAY

4

Where do you put your faith, and where would one deduce you put your faith if one were to observe the way you live your life?

DAY

5

What aspects of the kingdom of God are most meaningful to you at present?

A person who is very productive and yet who knows how to relax once said, "People see what I have accomplished and ask me how I do it. Some even tell me to slow down. The truth be told—I like my life. I'm not busy; I'm fruitful. And there's a difference. I see tangible results from my effort, and I am fulfilling my purpose in life. I am having a blast!"

Use this worksheet to gain perspective on where all your 168 hours are going. You will gain much if you do an honest assessment of the way you spend your time. How much time do you actually set aside to keep your eternal perspective clear?

Using this pie-shaped circle, make a rough pie chart of how you spend a typical week. The activities list on the left will get you started. Add or subtract categories to suit your normal week.

HOURS   ACTIVITY

_____	workplace
_____	family/friends
_____	sleep
_____	hygiene
_____	meals
_____	housekeeping
_____	church-related
_____	exercise/health
_____	reflection/devotion
_____	entertainment
_____	_____
_____	_____

168   **TOTAL**

Uded by permission. www.insidework.net/webfiles/downloads/products/168hr-worksheet.pdf

As you cast an eye toward the future, here are some "out-of-the-box" retirement plan ideas, in no particular order:

1. Become financially secure so that you can spend the rest of your life traveling the world, freely encouraging people with the gifts, talents, and experiences God has given you.
2. Purchase a beautiful lodge on the Mediterranean coast or some other exotic locale so that you can provide a place for missionaries to recharge their batteries.
3. Travel around North America, raising the funds necessary to ship containers of relief supplies to other countries in need of basic medical equipment/medicines, computers, clothing, etc.
4. Become a part of SCORE, an organization designed for seniors who can mentor people starting out in business.
5. Learn how to start or support established microfinancing projects designed to fund responsible entrepreneurs in developing nations.

Discussion Questions from Chapter Twelve in the Book and More:

1. Reflect on the ups and downs of your personal history. Make a list of all the positive wisdom lessons you have learned from these adventures.

2. Identify your biggest critics over the years. What, if anything, have you learned from your critics? Write a thank-you letter to each critic, which may help clarify any personal lessons you have learned. You know the issues—you may or may not be inclined to mail the letters. It's your decision. I remember hearing an eighty-eight-year-old man say, "I have outlived all my critics, and I have outloved all my enemies." Some day, I'd like to say something like that, wouldn't you?

3. According to Romans 5:1–5, why do you think God allows hardships into a person's life?

4. List and discuss three things about heaven that make any suffering you have experienced here on earth worthwhile.

5. If you have the assurance that God has a plan for your life, you will see all that comes into your life as the outworking of his grand design. He is the master weaver, and we see the tapestry of life as seemingly tangled threads from the reverse side. He sees the beautiful pattern he is working in and through us. What do you think the tapestry looks like from God's point of view?

THOUGHTS ON FINANCES AND THE BIBLE FROM A CERTIFIED FINANCIAL PLANNER™:

Check *Week Thirteen* in the appendix.

Prayer: "Lord, I sometimes get so caught up with what's happening in my own world that I forget the eternal perspective. Help me gain a much clearer view of who you are and how you work in the lives of those who trust you. Help me process the information in this workbook so that I can give my customers and coworkers a clearer view of you. May my words and deeds always communicate that I truly believe that heaven is real."

THE NON-PROFIT FACTOR

Ancient Wisdom

Proverbs 16:9: "In his heart a man plans his course, but the LORD determines his steps."

Proverbs 16:16: "How much better to get wisdom than gold, to choose understanding rather than silver!"

Proverbs 19:2: "It is not good to have zeal without knowledge, nor to be hasty and miss the way."

Proverbs 30:8: "Give me neither poverty nor riches, but give me only my daily bread."

Reflections

As you read chapter thirteen in the book, what were your initial thoughts and feelings about what you were reading (positive and/or negative)?

If you were able to communicate with the author while reading this chapter, what would you have said?

What were some thoughts (if any) you had about connecting the contents of this particular chapter to your business enterprise?

Additional Perspectives

Some rhetorical questions: What if your emc^2 group was the main catalyst behind the development or the expansion of the intercultural global mission's outreach of your church? What if a small portion of the money each group member makes is set aside collectively as a matching scholarship fund that initially permits a few members of your church to go out on a short-term mission trip?

The matching funds goal can grow from granting funds for a few to providing a matching scholarship for many members of your church. I hope that the following information will foster an honest discussion in your group about this or another similar plan to collectively bless others.

Whenever a church congregation decides to send a mission team to another country, there is always the question: "But why are we sending a mission team to another part of the world when there are crack addicts and other dire needs within a radius of three miles around our own church?"

The answer to that question is found in Acts 1:8: "But ye shall receive power, after the Holy Ghost is come upon you: and ye shall be witnesses unto me *both* in Jerusalem, and in all Judea, and in Samaria, *and* unto to the uttermost part of the earth" (KJV, emphasis added).

The key words are "both" and "and," indicating a simultaneous vision. In my studied opinion, every local church has the biblical mandate to reach out *both* locally/regionally *and* internationally. Obedience to the biblical mandate has its rewards. The international outreach impacts the local/regional vision in unimaginable ways. Many pastors have stated that sending teams to other countries has helped purify the message and the spirit of their local congregation.

Bottom Line. When a team comes back from a mission trip, its enthusiasm is catching. It's hard to put into words, but the reported result (in the local "sending" church) is less gossip, less pettiness, less politics, and more of a passion for the real needs of people within a square mile of the church. "Some like to live within the sound of a church bell. I'd rather run a rescue shop within a yard of hell," said C. T. Studd.

It is my heartfelt prayer that this information can be an encouragement to hundreds of churches. It seems like the Holy Spirit is stirring many churches to move more intentionally toward actively participating in intercultural missions. Writing checks to help missions is wonderful and a valid use of funds, but it is truly rewarding when we develop face-to-face, heart-to-heart, intercultural relationships that last a lifetime.

What if every church impacted by this workbook ultimately caught the vision to give the opportunity for every member of its congregation to go out on a short-term mission trip? Some may even develop a long-term commitment to a specific country.

A friend recently mentioned, "The call to go and make disciples of all nations has already been given in the Bible (Matthew 28:18–20). Each Christian must receive the specific call from God to stay!" Words worth pondering.

"Some pray; some give; some go" is a common response, and this statement contains a measure of truth. It is my dream that everyone (who is physically able) can experience at least one short-term mission trip in his or her lifetime, regardless of age. It's a life-changing experience! I would challenge every emc[2] member to go on a mission trip first, to experience the personal impact from such an adventure.

Please review the "Intercultural Global Mission's Philosophy" in the appendix section of this workbook for more detailed information. Spend some time pondering this material.

DAY
1

Does your family recognize the authenticity of your life? In what measurable ways?

DAY
2

What is the next book you are going to read? Why that particular book?

DAY
3

Do you have a quiet center to your life? What does it mean to have a quiet center?

DAY
4

Is integrity in the small matters built into your reflexes? How are you aware of this? When was the last time you caught yourself living with integrity . . . with no one watching?

DAY
5

List two occasions when your inner life was very different from your outer life. What were the causes? How have you coped with this difference?

For some emc^2 members, going to a Perspectives seminar might be the next logical step (check out the website www.Perspectives.org for the next Perspectives session in your area). Discuss some ideas on how your church-related entrepreneur club can have a higher purpose for existence. This could be the greater reason for your existence.

Permit me to switch the channel for a moment. We can easily compartmentalize our Christianity. "I'm not in ministry. I work seventy hours a week on building my business. Pastors and missionaries are examples of those in full-time ministry. Some day I might be able to get into full-time ministry."

There is no difference between the secular and the sacred. Everything that is moral and ethical is sacred. Playing sports is sacred. Cooking a meal for your family is sacred. Playing a game of checkers with one of your kids in the living room is sacred. Your business is sacred. This is one of your God-given assignments for this time in your life.

How many long-term missionaries, soup kitchen ministries, and genuine outreach ministries to unwed mothers, teenagers, or drug addicts spend a lot of their time raising funds? Wouldn't it be wonderful to link them up with people God has gifted with smart business sense so that they could spend the lion's share of their time fulfilling the assignment God has given them to do?

Everybody has an assignment. For entrepreneurs it's a special assignment: looking for ways to grow the business (making lots of money), without losing the eternal perspective, and then looking to prayerfully and financially support people who have trained all their lives to fulfill their God-given assignments locally or abroad. It's especially fun when you have personally witnessed the dedication of such people. You know that you are giving your hard-earned money to a verifiable, excellent ministry. If you don't know of anyone who fits that description, contact me, and I can point you to a number of people who are behind-the-scenes heroes of the faith, who spend every penny with wisdom, with God as their audience.

Consider this: Establish a reasonable, ongoing lifestyle for your family, pay off all your bills, set aside enough money for your children's education and inheritance. Then, look for ways to give away the rest to people and organizations that are doing God's work with integrity and fiscal responsibility. I think that this concept just might put a big fat smile on the face of Jesus. We'll see . . .

Discussion Questions from Chapter Thirteen in the Book and More:

1. When it comes to giving back to the community, what is your passion?

2. Start dreaming about it. Be bold enough to create a non-profit organization even when you aren't making much money. Watch the dream develop over time.

3. How can you connect your family and/or friends to the concept of a non-profit vision? *Hint*: Let them help you develop the mission statement, core values, etc. If they help you plan it, they will take "ownership" of the vision. And if they "own" the non-profit vision with you, they will help you take care of it. Don't rush into this. Take your time, letting everyone close to you touch it along the way.

4. If you agree with the "Intercultural Global Mission's Philosophy" in the appendix section, why do you agree? If you disagree with the information, why?

5. Make a list of the ways your emc² group can start or enhance the missions outreach of your church. Here's a starter idea: Check out the website about *Everyday Matters® Magazine* (OutreachMag.com), professionally designed to help develop a relevant outreach tool for your church, along with an opportunity for business owners in your congregation and community to advertise their respective goods and services. Who in your group would like to spearhead this idea?

6. Make a list of the people or ministries that are genuinely fulfilling their God-given assignments and that your group may want to eventually support on a regular basis.

THOUGHTS ON FINANCES AND THE BIBLE FROM A CERTIFIED FINANCIAL PLANNER™:

Check *Week Fourteen* in the appendix.

Prayer: "Lord, please show me how my business can be used by you to reach others with the good news of the gospel. I want to leave a legacy that will last for eternity. Show me how to be even more successful in my business so that I can give more money away to causes that will help others to hear about the good news of your death, burial, and resurrection. Your Word and people's souls are two things that will last forever. May I invest my life in those two things."

WHO'S COVERING YOUR BLIND SPOT?

Ancient Wisdom

Proverbs 16:20: "Whoever gives heed to instruction prospers, and blessed is he who trusts in the Lord."

Proverbs 18:13: "He who answers before listening—that is his folly and his shame."

Proverbs 26:16: "The sluggard is wiser in his own eyes than seven men who answer discreetly."

Matthew 6:1: "Be careful not to do your 'acts of righteousness' before men, to be seen by them. If you do, you will have no reward."

Reflections

As you read chapter fourteen in the book, what were your initial thoughts and feelings about what you were reading (positive and/or negative)?

If you were able to communicate with the author while reading this chapter, what would you have said?

What were some thoughts (if any) you had about connecting the contents of this particular chapter to your business enterprise?

Additional Perspectives

Dreams are fragile and need the same tender nurturing that a vulnerable baby requires in its early months of life. There are plenty of ways a dream can die. Pressure comes from all sides: financial, relational, spiritual, and much more. Criticism can be one of the biggest challenges. Criticism from people who don't know us can hurt, but the criticism from friends and family can create the kind of dream-crushing pressure that hits us in our most vulnerable areas.

To better understand the concept of dream-crushing pressure and how to deal with it, let's take a look at the fish at the bottom of the ocean and learn. Science reporter April Holladay writes,

> The deepest place in the ocean (the Mariana Trench) is about 100 miles (160km) southwest of Guam. The trench bottom lies 6.8 miles (11,000m) below the sea's surface—farther below sea level than Mount Everest is above sea level. Water pressure there is over a thousand times greater than at sea level. Until 1960, no man had ever dived that deep. On January 23, U.S. Navy Lt. Don Walsh and Swiss oceanic engineer

Jacques Piccard took the U.S. Navy bathyscaphe *Trieste* down. Gravity pulled *Trieste*, loaded with iron shot, to the bottom of the Mariana Trench. She dropped into growing darkness. A soft thump, four hours later, and she was down.. . . Peering out the 2.5-inch (6.35cm) porthole and probing total darkness with his spotlight, Piccard saw a flat fish (about a foot long) on the bottom just before they landed. Perhaps a type of flounder or perch. That's the deepest fish ever sighted—as deep as the ocean gets.

The question could be asked, "How can a fish handle the several-tons-per-square-inch, bone-crushing pressure at the bottom of the ocean?"

Holladay responds to such a question with, "The trick is to keep the pressure inside the fish the same as that outside. Only pressure difference can crush. So, if the difference is essentially zero, the fish is OK. Fish tissue is at about the same pressure as the outside pressure and thus balancing everything out."

Let's come up out of the ocean and take a look at life where we live. Scientists at NASA tell us that the earth's atmosphere is pressing against each square inch of our bodies with a force of 1 kilogram per square centimeter (approximately 14.7 pounds per square inch). The force on 1,000 square centimeters (a little larger than a square foot) is about a ton!

Why doesn't all that air pressure crush us? Here's a plausible response. The air *inside* our bodies balances out the pressure from outside so we don't implode. The pressure from the outside is just enough so that we don't explode.

God designed the perfect balance of internal and external pressure for his creation so that life could exist anywhere on our planet. What's the point? This is also true with criticism and other types of crushing compression that can squeeze the very life out of you and your entrepreneurial dreams.

When, not if, you feel external pressure, that's the time to figure out what kind of matching pressure is on the inside so that you don't implode with procrastination, negativity, and emotional/mental/spiritual paralysis.

God has also designed the perfect balance in the spiritual realm. Prayer, praise, worship, gratitude, repentance, regular study/meditation on the Word of God, and the filling of the Holy Spirit are ways to develop the inner strength, which helps you deal with the external issues that are designed to

DAY 1

In seven words describe yourself. What image do these words portray about you?

DAY 2

Name three to five of the most influential people in your life. In what areas and in what ways have they mentored or influenced you?

DAY 3

Write a brief sketch of the remainder of your life. List at least fifteen things you want to accomplish before you die. Carry that list in your wallet, checking off items as you accomplish them.

DAY

4

What actions do you now need to take based on your responses to the previous thirty days of self-coaching questions? Make a list in order of importance. Set deadlines, and cross off items as you achieve them. If you miss a deadline, reset it and try again. Don't quit!

DAY

5

What parallels do you see between the use of time (spending hours) and the use of money (spending money)?

BONUS

What is the toughest question you have ever been asked? How did you respond at the time? How would you respond to the same question now?

crush your spirit.

Discussion Questions from Chapter Fourteen in the Book and More:

1. Who are the most negative people in your life right now? If any have been identified, what can you learn from them? Or is there anything to be learned?

2. Is there at least one person with whom you feel comfortable enough to ask to be an objective mentor to you? If so, invite him or her to give you the "unvarnished" truth at all times. Bounce unformed ideas, and ask for any cautionary thoughts or words of wisdom.

3. Author and "blind spot" expert Claudia Shelton states that there are five common blind spot categories that can plague successful people. Review the five categories, illustrate each with personal experiences, and then discuss how each blind spot can negatively impact your business enterprise and how to deal with it:
   a. Misused Strengths: A strength you use too little or too much.
   b. Old Habits: Relying on behaviors that made you successful in the past that are no longer effective.
   c. Stress Expressed: How your behavior under stress affects others in ways you are unaware.
   d. Untuned Radar: Ignoring the nonverbal cues you give and receive.
   e. Disconnect: Ignoring factors important to effective communication.

4. How does the example of fish dealing with the extreme pressure at the bottom of the ocean help you increase the amount of time you dedicate to enriching your inner life? What do you do on a regular basis to enhance your personal development?

5. If you are a kite, who is holding your string, helping to keep you grounded? Describe your relationships with the "string holders" in your life. Are there any changes you need to make in your attitude

toward them? If so, what? And how are you going to communicate your thoughts and feelings to them?

THOUGHTS ON FINANCES AND THE BIBLE FROM A CERTIFIED FINANCIAL PLANNER™:
Check *Week Fifteen* in the appendix.

Prayer: "Lord, use your Word as a mirror to help me see my blind spots. Help me find one or two other wise individuals who will help me both personally and professionally to develop a full 360-degree perspective on my life. And may I not shrink back from maintaining an honest and open relationship with the Holy Spirit on all counts."

SWOT ANALYSIS

Ancient Wisdom

Proverbs 11:30: "The fruit of righteousness is a tree of life, and he who wins souls is wise."

Proverbs 12:1: "Whoever loves discipline loves knowledge, but he who hates correction is stupid."

Proverbs 16:11: "Honest scales and balances are from the LORD; all the weights in the bag are of his making."

Proverbs 28:13: "He who conceals his sins does not prosper, but whosoever confesses and renounces them finds mercy."

Reflections

As you read this section of the book, what were your initial thoughts and feelings about what you were reading (positive and/or negative)?

If you were able to communicate with the author while reading this section, what would you have said?

What were some thoughts (if any) you had about connecting the contents of this particular section of the book to your business enterprise?

Additional Perspectives

"Abraham left, not knowing whither . . ." (see Hebrews 11:8). Abraham was not some kind of nomad. Archaeological findings inform us of the fact that Ur was a very progressive place. Abraham moved on, leaving the comforts of his home in Ur, with no idea where he was going. No business plan. No financial plan. No marketing plan. No SWOT analysis.

On the other hand, we see scriptural support for developing a concrete plan as to what we are doing, why we are doing it, and how we are going to do it. Jesus stated, "Which of you, intending to build a tower, does not sit down first and count the cost, whether he has enough to finish it?" (Luke 14:28 NKJV).

What might have been required in counting the cost? A business plan? A financial plan? A SWOT analysis?

Some people tend to skew one way or the other—toward faith or toward the task. Think about it. Discuss it. What part does your personality style play? What is your conclusion on faith and works and how all this can impact the entrepreneurial journey?

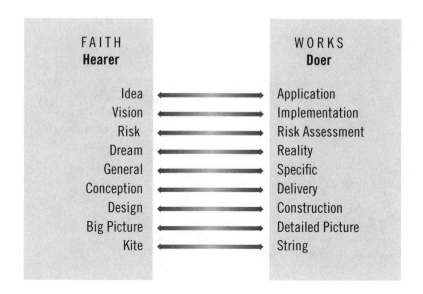

FAITH **Hearer**		WORKS **Doer**
Idea	⟷	Application
Vision	⟷	Implementation
Risk	⟷	Risk Assessment
Dream	⟷	Reality
General	⟷	Specific
Conception	⟷	Delivery
Design	⟷	Construction
Big Picture	⟷	Detailed Picture
Kite	⟷	String

There are two aspects that provide a balance for life.

FAITH

Abraham

"Now the LORD had said to Abram:

'Get out of your country, from your family and from your father's house, to a land that I will show you. I will make you a great nation; I will bless you and make your name great; and you shall be a blessing. I will bless those who bless you. And I will curse him who curses you; And in you all the families of the earth shall be blessed.' So Abram departed as the Lord had spoken to him . . ." (Genesis 12: 1–4 NKJV).

"By faith Abraham obeyed when he was called out to the place which he would receive as an inheritance. And he went out, not knowing where he was going" (Hebrews 11:8 NKJV).

WORKS

James

"What *does* it profit, my brethren, if someone says he has faith but does not have works? . . . faith by itself, if it does not have works is dead" (James 2:14–17 NKJV).

"But be doers of the word, and not hearers only, deceiving yourselves" (James 1:22 NKJV).

Building a Tower

"Which of you, intending to build a tower, does not sit down first and count the cost, whether he has *enough* to finish it—lest, after he has laid the foundation, and is not able to finish, all who see *it* begin to mock him, saying, 'This man began to build and was not able to finish'" (Luke 14:28–30 NKJV).

FAITH	WORKS
Noah	**Going to War**
"And God said to Noah. . . . Make yourself an ark of gopherwood; make rooms in the ark, and cover it inside and outside with pitch" (Genesis 6:13–14 NKJV).	"Or what king, going to make war against another king, does not sit down first to consider whether he is able with ten thousand to meet him who comes against him with twenty thousand?" (Luke 14:31 NKJV).
"Now faith is the substance of things hoped for and the evidence of things not seen" (Hebrews 11:1 NKJV).	
"But without faith it is impossible to please Him . . ." (Hebrews 11:6 NKJV).	

Discussion Questions from the Book and More:

Explore your entrepreneurial pursuit from the perspective of the SWOT (Strengths, Weaknesses, Opportunities, and Threats) analysis chart found on pages 162–163 of the workbook.

Carrying out this analysis will often be illuminating—in terms of both pointing out what needs to be done and putting problems into perspective.

The creator of the SWOT method is not known, but it is a technique that began to become popular for business strategic planning in the 1960s and then was adapted for broader use in many other fields where strategic planning was needed.

Prayer: "Lord, help me understand what it means to walk by faith and also what it means to count the cost. You know which way I tend to skew. I do not want to be driven by a lack of faith. Neither do I want to be driven by the need to make sure that everything is in order before taking the first step of obedience. Please give me the wisdom to know what is needed when. I am putty in your hands."

Strengths: (Build on Them)	**W**eaknesses: (Resolve Them)
What are your advantages?	What could be improved?
What do you do well?	What do you do badly?
Why did you decide to enter the field you did?	What should you avoid?
	What do you do poorly or not at all?
What were the motivating factors and influences?	What objections do potential clients frequently raise?
What relevant resources do you have?	What are your professional weaknesses?
What do other people see as your strengths?	How do these weaknesses affect your job performance? (These might include weakness in technical skill areas or in leadership or interpersonal skills.)
Do these factors still represent some of your inherent strengths?	
What need do you expect to fill within your organization?	Think about your most unpleasant experiences in school or in past jobs, and consider whether some aspect of your personal or professional life could be a root cause.
What have been your most notable achievements?	
To what do you attribute your success?	
How do you measure your success?	
What knowledge or expertise will you bring to the company you join that may not have been available to the organization before?	NOTE: Consider this from an internal and external basis. Do other people seem to perceive weaknesses that you do not see? It is best to be realistic now, and face any unpleasant truths as soon as possible.
What is your greatest asset?	
NOTE: Consider this from your own point of view and from the point of view of the people you deal with. Don't be modest—be realistic. If you are having any difficulty with this, try writing down a list of your characteristics. Some of these will hopefully be strengths!	

The leftmost column reads vertically: **INTERNAL FACTORS**

Opportunities: (Exploit Them)	**T**hreats: (Avoid Them)
What are the promising prospects facing you?	What threatens the current personal & organizational growth?
What are the best opportunities in the near future?	What obstacles do you face?
	Are the requirements for your desired job field changing?
What is the "state of the art" in your particular area of expertise?	
	Could any of your weaknesses seriously threaten your business?
Are you doing everything you can to enhance your exposure to this area?	Who is your competition and what are they doing well?
What formal training and education can you add to your credentials that might position you appropriately for more opportunities?	Does changing technology threaten your prospective position?
	What is the current trend line for your personal area of expertise?
Would an MBA or another graduate degree add to your advantage?	
	Could your area of interest be fading in comparison to more emergent fields?
How quickly are you likely to advance in your chosen career?	
	Is there a bad debt or cash flow problem?
List changes in government policy related to your field?	
	Is your chosen field subject to internal politics that will lead to conflict?
What are the interesting trends: such as changes in social patterns, media, technology (macro/micro), economy, population profiles, lifestyle changes, etc.?	
	Is there any way to change the politics or to defuse your involvement in potential disputes?
	How might the economy negatively affect your future company and your work group?
NOTE: One useful approach when looking at opportunities is to look at your strengths and ask yourself whether these open up any opportunities. Alternatively, look at your weaknesses and ask yourself whether you could open up opportunities by eliminating them.	Will your future company provide enough access to new challenges to keep you sharp—and marketable—in the event of sudden unemployment?

The left margin of the table reads vertically: EXTERNAL FACTORS

APPENDIX

Your Work and the Bible

Work can sometimes drag us down. But that's not its original, God-given intention. God designed work to help you share your unique talents with others and form a balanced community, as well as enjoy the fruits of your labor well done.

How do you keep a biblical perspective and purpose in life when everything conspires to blow you off your spiritual foundations? We need to recover the biblical rhythm of rest in the midst of our business. What is the antidote to the life-sucking force of modern work and life? Learn the joyful, life-renewing difference that longs to be integrated into life.

The following overview provides a brief description of various topics with the Scriptures that, if applied, can help us gain an enhanced biblical perspective. For more comprehensive articles on each topic, go to ChristianityToday.com/biblestudies/ features/work.html.

How can I handle the competing demands of home and work?

- Work during the week—but leave weekends for worship and recreation. Exodus 23:10–13

- Put God first in every area of your life. Deuteronomy 6:1–9

- Focus your eyes on God. 2 Samuel 1

- Plan a getaway. Matthew 14:22, 23

How can I have healthy relationships with [my coworkers]?

- Be someone your coworkers can count on. Esther 4

- Keep appropriate sexual boundaries. Proverbs 5

- Treat coworkers as brothers and sisters. Romans 12:9–18

- Help each other live by God's purposes. Galatians 6:1–10

How can I rise above office politics?

- Hold yourself above gossip and jealousy. Deuteronomy 5:20, 21

- Put yourself at risk if it will prevent harm to others. Esther 7:1–6

- Remember who you are. Matthew 20:20–28

- Realize you're free—to respond with love. Galatians 5:13–16

- Recognize your master is God. Colossians 3:22–4:1

- Don't overrate the in-crowd. James 3:5–18

Sometimes I think it's okay to work while my kids are young; other times I'm not sure. How can I be certain I'm making the best decision for my family?

- Check the motives behind your decision. Proverbs 16:1–3

- Seek God's wisdom in your decision. Romans 14:13–23

- Make sure your priorities align with Scripture. Titus 2:3–8

My spouse is sometimes threatened by my career. How should I respond?

- Try these steps for dealing with jealousy. Numbers 12
- Focus on Christ's power, not your own. Luke 3:7–20
- Respect your own and your spouse's skills as gifts from God. 1 Corinthians 12:1–11

How can I find satisfaction with my life outside of work?

- Aim for balance in how you use time. Ecclesiastes 3:1–14
- Accept God's invitation. Isaiah 55:1–5
- Realize your value doesn't depend on what you do but on who God is. Deuteronomy 8:10–20

How can I deal with a dishonest coworker?

- Stay true to yourself—and don't doubt God's power. Psalm 26
- Set an example by your own honesty and integrity. Proverbs 28:11–26
- Honor God in the way you do business. Amos 2
- Remember, dishonesty often brings its own punishment. Habakkuk 2:4–17

Sometimes my male colleagues don't take me seriously. How can a woman be assertive at work without being offensive?

- Trust God to bring good even from acts intended to harm. Genesis 50:15–21

- When given opportunity to lead, do it well. Judges 4:4–15

- Learn to lead. Isaiah 11:1–9

- Demonstrate your talents with integrity and humility. Ephesians 5:6–21

How can I be a good supervisor?

- Pick capable people and give them clearly defined responsibilities. Exodus 18

- Listen to God. 1 Kings 3:5–15; 4:29–34

- Manage conflicts by focusing on what's really important. Ezra 5:1–6:12

- Lead by example. Jeremiah 32:26–44

- Be gracious about the imperfections of others. John 21:15–25

- Help other people flourish. 2 Timothy 1:1–7

- Correct the mistake; forgive the person. Philemon 8–16

- Don't let position get to your head. Philemon 15–25

How can I be more confident about my work?

- God always equips you to do what He calls you to do. Deuteronomy 31:1–6

- God is always with you. Joshua 1:1–9

- God is your strength. Psalm 73:21–28

- God is your silent partner at work. Psalm 108

- Obedience to God leads to confidence. 1 John 3:19–24

Can I do the "Lord's work" in a [general-market job]? If so, how?

- Examine who you are at work. 1 Samuel 14:1–15

- Try to enjoy the work you have or find work that you enjoy. Ecclesiastes 2:24–26

- Listen for God's voice. Matthew 4:18–22

- Let God work from the inside out. Matthew 15:10–20

What's a good way for me to share my faith at work?

- Remember, you are an earthen vessel—with treasure inside. 2 Corinthians 4:1–15

- Earn the respect of your coworkers. 1 Thessalonians 4:9–12

- Be honest, respectful, and fair—just as if you were in church. 1 Timothy 5:17–6:2

- Bring your faith up naturally when it's appropriate. 2 Timothy 1:6–14

Intercultural Global Mission's Philosophy

My philosophy on missions has been shaped by intensive study in the Word, prayer, travels around the world to well over fifty countries and a simple determination to obey the simultaneous vision outlined in Acts 1:8: Jerusalem, Judea and Samaria (town/city, county, state/province, region), and the uttermost part of the world.

One of the things I avoid like the plague is the somewhat typical ugly North American approach. Even though we may not be conscious of it, we may project this attitude: *"We're rich; you're poor. We're strong; you're weak. We're smart and you're . . . well . . . not so smart."* It's this type of paternalistic, patronizing attitude that I reject.

But this kind of an attitude can so easily and almost unconsciously creep into our mindset regarding intercultural missions. This type of mindset can even creep into our North American outreaches—suburban church reaching out to urban church. I have had to confront this thinking in my own heart and mind.

A short-term mission trip occupies a wonderful niche when it comes to evangelism. It is especially designed for people who want to get their feet wet in missions. While I thank God for short-term missions, I believe that we can develop a long-term partnership with an indigenous (developing nation) church that is based upon relationship, flexibility, integrity, and mutual respect.

Wouldn't it be wonderful if your emc² club could be the prime "shaking and moving" organization within your church? When I was a pastor (1975–1993), we developed a model that I believe may work very well in your church. (It's up to you to provide the connectors to your church.) Here are some of the wisdom lessons we learned:

1. The developing-nation church is encouraged to address the spirit-soul-body aspects of the Christian message on its own, without looking to a rich North American sugar daddy to bail it out of its financial and structural challenges. This establishes a Christ-centered relationship vs. a need-centered relationship. And, by the way, North Americans generally possess the need to give. It just manifests itself in a more socially acceptable manner. The need to

be needed can be a powerful intoxicant. This can be an inhibitor to building genuine relationships, and this inordinate need to do some special project will get smoked out during the process.

2. The North American church is encouraged to "cool its jets"—to not foster the idea that it is going to immediately build a clinic, fix something, or dig a well. This builds patience, teachability, and humility. We think we are going to give. But in the midst of the process we realize that we are receiving much more than we are giving. The developing-nation church we are "ministering to" generally has a depth in Jesus we have never experienced. Here is a suggestion: The first year is dedicated to developing a solid relationship with the church members. The first year may include digging a well, because sometimes excellent relationships are developed when everyone is sweating. But the most important aspect is to build a relationship where both entities are coming from the position of strength.

3. Two times a year can be dedicated to sending teams over to the country of choice. Perhaps a team can be sent every spring and every fall. Twelve years of age is the youngest person I have ever taken on a short-term mission trip. At that age it is a case-by-case situation. Some kids are more mature than others at that age. Some may say, *"That kid is probably going on this trip just because of the excitement of traveling to another country."* My response? I couldn't care less about the motivation of some who are going on the trip. I just want them to go with a team of people who want to serve the Lord. God has a way of challenging and changing lives regardless of the initial motivation for going—even those who went with the "right" motivation! A good friend (Phillip Sims) once said, "Instead of motivating to mobilize, mobilize to motivate." Take the time to really think about that statement—and how it can relate to how you communicate your vision for missions.

Every team will have to commit to pretravel training and then will have debriefing for a couple of weeks after it comes back to smoke out any reverse culture shock issues. Each team can present a short slide or video presentation at a Sunday morning church service so that the entire congregation feels a part of the entire mission. The goal will be to provide the opportunity for everyone to at least dream about going on one of the trips. This ongoing mission will impact the fervency, the passion for the lost, and the prayer life of the church. It has a way of purifying the spirit of a church like few things can. I have witnessed it up close and personal.

4. As a part of the church's missions budget, a church can develop a

scholarship plan. I do not believe in giving freebies to people. There has to be some character-building sweat equity. This alone helps to expand personal faith and perseverance. When I pastored a church, we matched 50 percent of the actual costs of airfare, ground travel, three meals a day, and lodging. All other costs were borne by the individual. For instance, roundtrip airfare may cost $600, while lodging, food, and ground travel may cost $60 a day for, let's say, ten days. That makes a grand total of $1,200 for the entire trip. The church matches the $600 that is raised by the individual. The local church's financial investment in these mission outreaches will pay dividends for years to come. And what a positive way to fight negativity, gossip, and foolishness! The perfect antidote for the small-mindedness that rules some churches.

For the youth, car washes and bake sales can be sponsored to provide avenues for them to raise funds. This type of use of church funds makes an incalculable investment in the lives of people in our church, which will impact many for the rest of their lives. Some people haven't even ventured more than fifty to a hundred miles from their homes in their lifetimes. Just the travel experience alone will open eyes and hearts. In 1869 Mark Twain said, *"Travel is fatal to prejudice, bigotry and narrow-mindedness and many of our people need it sorely on those accounts. Broad, wholesome, charitable views of men and things cannot be acquired by vegetating in one little corner of the earth all one's lifetime."* I agree.

5. Some North American churches are getting into a global mindset for the first time. I encourage those churches to think about going to an English-speaking country like Jamaica, Barbados, or Belize. Why? Because so many more people in the congregation can feel a part of what is happening. A language barrier provides its own wonderful cross-cultural experiences, but I am thinking that a common language can provide many more ministry opportunities for more people. Try the Ladder Method:

- 1st Rung: Develop an awareness of the need for global missions. Send some members of the congregation to a missions conference.

- 2nd Rung: Start praying for different countries around the world. *Operation World* and *WindoWatchman* are two excellent resources.

- 3rd Rung: Invite missions-minded speakers to your church to communicate on the topic of global missions.

- 4th Rung: Develop the mission, vision, core values, operating principles of your church that include the simultaneous vision of both Jerusalem, Judea and Samaria, and the uttermost part of the earth.

- 5th Rung: Send a small group of leaders from the church to a country on a kind of a reconnaissance mission to check out the viability of the church's involvement in global missions.

- 6th Rung: Send your first short-term team, and then see how God will expand the missions perspective in your church.

- 7th Rung: Continue to keep hearts tender toward Jesus and to keep the eternal perspective in clear view.

Spend some time pondering this section. Discuss some ideas on how your entrepreneur club can have a higher purpose for existence.

Finding a Mentor/Becoming a Mentor

Serial entrepreneur, investor, and author (*Beyond Code*) Rajesh Setty states, "There is a good chance that you don't have a mentor right now and are not even considering entering into such a relationship in the near future. Yet athletes have mentors, actors have mentors, and business leaders have mentors. Why not you?" Read and then discuss the ten reasons Rajesh suggests that will encourage you to consider engaging a mentor:

1. The structure provides automatic accountability.

I have three mentors and I am fortunate for having each one of them. This always happens: A few days before my meeting with each of my mentors, I start attending to several of my pending matters. My mentors don't even have to ask me about things I promised to act on. I will take care of these things because I want to be ready with a "good" answer if they do ask me. The mentoring relationship, in a way, has built-in accountability.

2. They may ask you questions that you may never ask yourself.

Sometimes you may put off answering some questions just because you can. You will do this even typically for questions where you know the answers are not pretty. By postponing asking the hard questions you are not solving any problem, you are just avoiding the short-term pain. Your mentor may not be so nice to you. He or she has no problem asking those hard questions and actually prompting you to start doing something about those questions.

3. You can learn to reflect.

A mentor does not have an alternate agenda except to help get the most out of you. So you never have to worry about any other side effects as you discuss your life and work issues. That in itself will let you open up and reflect on things at a level that you have never seen before.

4. Discover the "real" problem and get help to solve it.

Sometimes we keep messing with symptoms rather than attacking the real problems. I have found time and again that I discuss a particular problem with my mentor and actually we end up solving the "real" problem. Solving the "real" problem will in turn solve the symptomatic problems that you first set out to solve.

5. You may escape from "short-term thinking."

Being in the technology world, you have no option but to be "current-buzz-word compliant" to ensure you are in the race. This means that you have to be running (hard) just to stay where you are. While this is great for short-term success, you can't ignore your long-term goals. Your mentor may help you balance the time you spend between short-term and long-term goals.

6. Get a "responsible" alternate perspective.

You may have other avenues where you can get alternate perspectives on a particular topic or issue. However, when a mentor provides an alternate perspective, there is a dose of responsibility that comes packaged with it. In other words, your mentor has a higher stake in the outcome than your peers and friends do.

7. Get into the "thinking" habit.

Every hour I spend with my mentors, my thinking will go to an overdrive mode. Most often, you get carried away and practice "thinking on the go"—meaning you will think while you are engaged in doing something. Mentoring will put a stop to that and start you on a "thinking" path. I am sure none of us will argue on the importance of the need to think.

8. Get ready to welcome new possibilities.

While everyone around you may be trying to "fix" things with you, your mentor will look at how you can capitalize on your strengths. Rarely can you claim to be aware of all your strengths. Even if you do, you may not be making the most of them. A mentor can work with you to ensure that you are spending most of your time in the areas of your strengths and also take care of other things (where you are not that good) by putting a suitable structure in place.

9. Learn to be in balance.

Mahatma Gandhi said, "One man cannot do right in one department of life whilst he is occupied in doing wrong in any other department. Life is one indivisible whole." While you may know this, being in the technology world, chances are that you may be neglecting several other parts of your life. With your mentor's help, you can be assured of living a more balanced life.

10. Get help to distinguish yourself in the marketplace.

Unless you distinguish yourself, you will be part of the commodity crowd. Not doing anything about it will only erode your value in the marketplace. Distinguishing yourself is a journey and not a destination. What is special today will no longer be special tomorrow. Your mentor can act as a catalyst here to help you rise above the commodity crowd quickly. If you are smart and disciplined, with or without a mentor you may succeed. Why not increase your odds by engaging with a mentor?

"Ten Good Reasons for Having a Mentor." Copyrighted by Rajesh Setty. Used with Permission. www.RajeshSetty.com.

Find a mentor. Become a mentor. Becoming a mentor completes the cycle of excellence in entrepreneurship. Giving back as a mentor to another person is the activity of expressing gratitude for all the mentors who have helped you on the road to success. Learn from the best, and then be the best mentor you can possibly be.

Thoughts on Finances and the Bible from a Certified Financial Planner™

Week One: Debt

When I was young, my father gave me a credit card with a very small limit. Since he was a financial planner, he was always trying to impart his wisdom to me through experience rather than just words. He placed a sticker on the top of the credit card that said, "WARNING: OVERUSE OF THIS CARD MAY BE HAZARDOUS TO YOUR WEALTH." He told me about how this card could be very convenient, as well as providing great benefits such as accumulating airline miles and other perks, but it could also cause problems if not used properly. I remember these words every time I want to buy something I shouldn't: "Pay off your bill every month; don't let the credit card company get rich off you."

The problem is not with the credit card, but it is with our lifestyle. God is very clear throughout the Bible about the importance of money and the dangers of debt. Proverbs 22:7 says, "The rich rule over the poor, and the borrower is servant to the lender." Do you really want to be enslaved to anyone or anything? I think not. It's against the nature of God and his gift of free will. God will not force you on this matter. It is up to us not to fall into the credit trap.

Questions and Study

1. Debt problems normally come from an inability to control our spending. We want it now, and we don't want to wait. Make a decision today to look at your budget. Go to your checkbook and credit cards, and write down everything that you have spent over the past three months. I think you will be amazed to see that a little discipline in your discretionary spending will greatly assist you in controlling your debt.
2. Psalm 37:21; Romans 13:8; Deuteronomy 28:15–16, 43–44; and Matthew 5:42. How do they relate to borrowing—especially the verse

in Psalm 37? I think it will make you think twice before taking on too much debt.

3. 1 Timothy 6:6. What does this verse say about being content with what we have? Can God really help control your spending? The question should be, Will you let him help you?

Week Two: To Trust What You Cannot See

It is hard to believe in something invisible—something that we can't see, touch, or feel. For the first twenty-two years of my life, I focused only on things that I could see. Since I could not see God directly in front of me, I had no reason to fellowship with him. Don't get me wrong, my parents raised me well and taught me about God, but I was not ready to truly believe that he was real. It took a few life-altering experiences as well as an amazing God-fearing woman (my wife) to believe in something I couldn't see with my eyes. That is where faith comes in, and we are not to rely upon our human understanding. Proverbs 3:5–6 says, "Trust in the LORD with all of your heart, and lean not on your own understanding; in all your ways acknowledge Him, and He shall direct your paths" (NKJV).

Saving and investing are very similar to this concept. Most of us are saving for our retirement. But what is retirement? For those who are not there yet, it is not something we can see, yet we continue to save for it because we have faith that if we are good stewards with our money we will be able to reap the rewards by one day enjoying our "golden years" in financial freedom.

Questions and Study

1. In what ways can the Bible and a relationship with God help us attain or maintain financial independence?
2. Did you know that one in every ten verses in the Bible refers in some way to finances/money? Look at a few of these to see for yourself: Proverbs 13:22; 21:20; 22:7; Luke 14:28; and Matthew 6:24.

Week Three: Gambling, the Stock Market, and Trying to Get Rich Quick

I was taught from a young age that anything in life that is worthwhile will not be easy. Also, if you want something, you must get up every day and work hard to obtain it. Many people today spend a lot of their time and money with get-rich-quick schemes. The biggest culprit is gambling. I am not referring just to Las Vegas casino-style gambling, but also the money spent on lottery tickets on a daily basis. Believe me, I would love to win one of those mega-million-dollar jackpots, but should I be investing my money in something that has the odds for success stacked against it?

The Bible has laid out instructions when it comes to these get-rich-quick schemes. Proverbs 28:22 says, "A man with an evil eye hastens after riches, and does not consider that poverty will come upon him" (NKJV). Many of us think that gambling is a game, but according to the Bible, it is a sin that will lead us to poverty.

The stock market also can be a form of gambling if you are trying to get rich quick. Many of you probably remember the dot-com days of the late 1990s, when people were making a tremendous amount of money in a short period of time. When the bottom dropped out in 2000, a lot of the wealth that had been created was wiped out very quickly. There is nothing wrong with investing in the stock market, and I believe it is one of the best ways to accumulate wealth, but it is not a get-rich-quick scheme. Two of the biggest mistakes you can make in the market are being greedy and being fearful. Many people invested in the market in the late '90s because they thought they could make a fortune overnight, but that is not what investing is all about. To invest, you must have a long-term vision and understand that the market will not make you rich quickly.

Questions and Study

1. Where are you investing your money? If you reside in the United States, your money may well be invested in a 401(k) or an IRA. Do you have a long-term focus or a short-term focus?
2. Look at Proverbs 13:11; what does it say about obtaining wealth?
3. If you do gamble or play the lottery, add up how much you spent last year and what you have to show for it. I would be surprised, actually

shocked, if more than a handful of people had greater gains than losses.

4. There is nothing like good old hard work and the regular investment of small amounts of money to build up your wealth.

Week Four: Investing

We all know that you can't take your riches with you when you die. I have never seen a moving van following a hearse. Having said that, I think the Bible is very clear about the importance of investing. I know God will take care of my needs, and I trust him with all my heart, but he did give me the ability to choose. We all should choose to prepare for the future. If you have accepted Christ as your personal Savior, then you know the importance of planning ahead. It is too late to wait to get to know God when you die. The Bible is clear that by believing in Christ and asking him into your heart you will go to heaven. Why then should we not plan for the future from a financial standpoint?

Proverbs 30:24–25 says, "There are four things which are little on the earth, but they are exceedingly wise: The ants are a people not strong, yet they prepare their food in the summer" (NKJV). God uses this illustration to show us how wise the ants are to prepare in the summer so they won't starve in the winter. This is the same for us when it comes to saving for things such as retirement and the education of our children.

Questions and Study

1. Proverbs 21:5 is direct about God's specific advice on investing. Will you heed his instructions? Study this verse, print it out, and put it someplace you can see it every day to remind you to save.

2. How much should you be saving for retirement? Most experts say you need at least 90 percent of your preretirement income. Go to a competent financial planner, and find out what it will take for you to retire.

3. My father always told others and me that if you are serious about retiring, then you should save at least 15 percent of your gross income every year. How much are you saving?

4. What does Jesus say in Luke 14:28 that would lead you to believe he feels that investing is important?

Week Five:
Leaving an Inheritance—Estate Planning

Many people are struggling just to finance their own retirements, let alone leave anything for their children. The Bible has many passages that talk about the importance of leaving an inheritance. By looking at Numbers 26:53–55; 27:1–11, you see God stressing the value of inheritance and the family. The passages talk mainly about land being transferred from one generation to the next, but I believe it can be applied to money and other material items. Proverbs 13:22 says, "A good man leaves an inheritance to his children's children" (NKJV).

I think the idea of inheritance can be looked at also as having properly planned your estate. While some of us may have amassed enough to live comfortably through retirement and leave a nice inheritance, that is only one part. We should have all of our legal documents in place before we die. I can't tell you how much money I have seen go to unnecessary taxes and expenses because people failed to plan. The United States government has an estate tax that in the year of this publication will take up to 45 percent of your estate over $2,000,000. I am not sure how this specific example connects with readers around the world. Even though your examples may be different, that is a lot of money that could have been saved. Also if you have children under the age of eighteen, do you want the courts to decide who will be their guardian, or would you rather leave instructions on whom you would want to take care of them? If you live in the United States, your IRAs, 401(k)s, and life insurance all have beneficiaries. Regardless where you reside, make sure you have the correct people receiving your money if you should pass.

Questions and Study

1. Consult with a competent estate-planning attorney. Do not try to plan your estate on your own.
2. Read 1 Kings 21:3–4 and Ezekiel 46:18. What do these passages say about inheritance?
3. If you don't have the following documents, make sure you follow item 1 above and get them completed: a durable power of attorney, a health-care power of attorney, a living will, and a will.

Week Six: Is Money the Root of All Kinds of Evil?

Many misquote the Bible and say that money itself is evil, but the verse says something very different. First Timothy 6:10 says, "For *the love of money* is a root of *all kinds* of evil, for which some have strayed from the faith in their greediness, and pierced themselves through with many sorrows" (NKJV, emphasis added). If someone is rich and has obtained a great deal of wealth, is that person now evil? Possessions say nothing about a person; it is what's in one's heart that counts. First Timothy 6:9 talks about the desire to be rich: "But those who desire to be rich fall into temptation and a snare, and into many foolish and harmful lusts which drown men in destruction and perdition" (NKJV).

When I was first starting out as a young broker at Merrill Lynch, I had one thing on my mind—to be rich. I worked extremely hard to have a nice car, a big home, and all the luxuries of having a lot of money. As I became more successful and earned more money, I found that I was less content than when I had nothing. My heart was in the wrong place because all I wanted was to earn more money. Once I accepted Christ as my Savior, my perspective on wealth began to change. Let me pause to say that I would be lying to say that I don't appreciate the material things that come along with being successful in my job, but now I try to put the emphasis on doing the right thing for my clients and help them achieve their goals and dreams. I believe that God showed me that by helping others first, success would follow. My heart needed to be in the right place.

Questions and Study

1. Have you ever looked inside your heart? It can be a scary thing sometimes. Look inside your heart, and find out what you want in life. Is it that nice car or big house? Or are you just praying that you will be able to pay next month's bills? Write down your goals and desires. You will quickly see which ones follow the heart of God. Remember, there is nothing wrong with having a goal to be successful and being able to afford nice things; the problem is when they become idols—replacing God as your primary focus in life.

2. In Deuteronomy 8:18, what does it say about where material blessings come from?

3. Read Luke 12:15 and see what Jesus is warning against.

Week Seven: Tithing

There are a number of biblically based perspectives on the topic of tithing. I am not going to try to talk anyone into my particular view on the topic, but I believe that tithing is a very crucial part of your walk with God. Most of us want to keep the money since we were the ones who earned it. But when we think about it, who gave us the passion, the intellect, the fingers, and the ability to sweat? Tithing can be viewed as a way of returning to our Creator a portion of what he has given us and allowed us to earn. A pastor at a church I used to attend gave one of the simplest illustrations of tithing. He had a bagful of potatoes, and he pulled out all ten of them, saying this is what God has given us. Then he placed one back in the bag and said this is all that God asks us to give back.

It is my opinion that the tithe (or "tenth") should be taken off the top of our income, meaning we should give 10 percent of our gross income, not our net. It should be treated like any other bill or tax. Most people would never consider not paying their mortgage, but some will not pay their entire bill to God. Actually, in Malachi 3:8 the Bible says that by not paying our tithes and offerings we are robbing God. I am not trying to be legalistic, but if you look at 2 Corinthians 9:7, you will see that God loves the cheerful giver: "So let each one give as he purposes in his heart, not grudgingly or of necessity; for God loves a cheerful giver" (NKJV). I have at times grudgingly pulled the checkbook out and given to an offering because I knew I was supposed to give. God wants us not to just give, but to want to give joyfully.

Some feel that they can't afford to give, but I would challenge them and say you can't afford *not* to give. The world's value system will always try to convince us that God's Word is fallible, but if we give, he has promised to provide. Look at Malachi 3:10: "'Bring all the tithes into the storehouse, that there may be food in My house . . . ,' says the LORD of hosts, 'If I will not open for you the windows of heaven and pour out for you such blessing that there will not be room enough to receive it" (NKJV). He is a God of promises. Will we trust that we will be financially content even if we give 10 percent of our income?

Questions and Study

1. Look at your income, and see if last year you gave 10 percent of your gross. If not, try to give more, but do so incrementally. For example, if you are giving 6 percent, make a goal of giving a full 10 percent by increasing your tithe each month so that within a few months you will be at the 10 percent level. You will probably not even notice it in your budget.

2. All contributions to non-profit organizations may be tax deductible, but you must keep a record of them and have evidence of any gift over $250. Ask your church to provide you a statement at the beginning of each year showing what you gave. You probably should be giving a check instead of cash since you can keep better record of what you have given.

3. Look at Deuteronomy 15:10. What a great promise!

Week Eight:
Having Wealth = Having Favor with God?

In Luke 16:19–31, Jesus tells the parable of the rich man and Lazarus. The rich man ended up in hell, while the beggar Lazarus was taken to heaven. In those days, it was a sign that God was favoring you if you had wealth and was punishing you if you were poor. Jesus told this parable to refute the idea that having money meant God loved you more. The rich man did not go to hell because of his wealth, but rather because of his evilness toward Lazarus.

Especially in American culture, those who have money are respected and put up on a pedestal. If Donald Trump were a poor man, no one would know his name. Now I am not saying that he is going to receive the same fate as the rich man in Luke, but those who do have wealth have a responsibility. Wealth should be viewed as a blessing and gift from God. This blessing, like any other, means we are to use it to carry out God's will, not our own. That is also why I love this country: because we are such a giving nation. The world may say that we are the evil Westerners and call us names, but when it comes to helping those less fortunate around the world, we are the number one philanthropists. We have been given much, and much is expected of us. In Luke 12:48 Jesus tells us this specifically: "But the one who does not know and does things deserving punishment will be beaten with few blows. From everyone who has been given much, much will be demanded; and from the one who has been entrusted with much, much more will be asked."

Questions and Study

1. Look in Mark 10:23–25 and see what it says about those who trust in their riches.
2. Pray daily for our country, for our leaders in the government, and for all citizens to continue to have giving hearts.
3. Read Deuteronomy 8:18, which talks about where material blessings come from.

Week Nine: Insurance

In Genesis 41 we see the story of Pharaoh's dreams. These dreams troubled his spirit, and he needed to know what they meant. He sent for magicians and wise men from all over the land of Egypt, but no one could interpret them. Finally a prisoner named Joseph was able to interpret the dreams. In verse 29, Joseph says that the dreams mean "indeed seven years of great plenty will come throughout all the land of Egypt; but after them seven years of famine will arise, and all the plenty will be forgotten in the land of Egypt; and the famine will deplete the land" (NKJV). Immediately Pharaoh began preparing for the coming famine by storing up enough food to feed his people.

Now the story of Pharaoh, and his dreams, is a great way to show us the importance of saving, but it also has a lot to do with having insurance. For example, I know a person who made a good deal of money while working, but when he was injured, he couldn't return to work. He had no disability insurance and went broke very quickly. We have to be very careful during the years of plenty so that we do not waste it, because there will come a time when we will have a famine in our lives. It could be the loss of a job, car accident, house fire, death of a spouse; or we could develop a serious health problem. By having the correct type and amount of insurance, we can manage our risks effectively. The most important aspect is that we managed our risks before they happen.

Questions and Study

1. Look at all of your insurance policies (life, health, disability, auto, homeowner's), and then figure out how much you will need. For life insurance, estimate how much your family and dependents would need if you were not around. For disability insurance, first, you need to have at least three to six months of your monthly budget as some type of reserve account, such as a money market or a certificate of deposit. Second, figure out how much income you would need if you were to become disabled and not able to work. Auto insurance is very important; make sure you look at your coverage for each accident and for each person. I also would recommend that you look at an umbrella liability policy. This would give you additional liability coverage on your home and your auto insurance policies.

2. Find a competent agent who can help you find the policy that is right for you. The above advice is for illustration purposes only and cannot be construed as specific financial advice. Again, please see your agent for help with your specific situation.

Week Ten: Asset Allocation

Asset allocation is the cornerstone to a proper investment strategy. The reason you allocate among various asset groups is because the best performing asset class varies and is very hard, almost impossible, to predict. Solomon, one of the richest men in history, gave us instructions on asset allocation. In Ecclesiastes 11:1–2 he states, "Send your grain across the seas, and in time, profits will flow back to you. But divide your investments among many places, for you do not know what risks might lie ahead" (NLT). In these verses he is telling us that we should invest, but make sure we don't put all our eggs in one basket. By allocating our money in different, noncorrelated assets we have the ability to reduce our risk. For many years during the 1980s and 1990s, the stock market produced outstanding returns, but the beginning of this century reminded people that with every up market there is inevitably a downside. The problem is not that the market decreased significantly; it is that many investors did not follow a proper asset-allocation plan. A good deal of the investing took place in the technology sector, which experienced some of the best returns and also the biggest losses. Had many people been more spread out in their investments, the bear market would not have taken so many victims.

Does this mean we should never invest? If you read on in verse 4 ("Farmers who wait for perfect weather never plant. If they watch every cloud, they never harvest" [NLT]), we see that there is no perfect time to invest. I was once told that "yesterday is history, tomorrow is a mystery, and today is a gift; that is why they call it the present."

Questions and Study

1. To craft a proper asset allocation, you must do the following about your investments:
    a. Find out what your risk tolerance is. If you stay awake at night thinking about your investments, perhaps the market is not the place for you.
    b. What are your objectives? Growth? Income? Both?
    c. How much time do you have to achieve your goals? Normally the less time, the less risk you should be taking; but young investors have the ability to take more risk because they are not depending upon their investments for income.
    Now take a look at your current investments: How much do you have in stocks? Bonds? Real estate? Cash? Does your current portfolio represent your risk tolerance, investment objectives, and time horizon? If not, then you should consider going to a financial professional such as a certified financial planner to see if you need to change your asset mix.
2. There have been many studies on asset allocation. To find out more, look at the work done by Harry Markowitz. Also, if you have a 401(k) or some type of employer-sponsored defined contribution plan, your employer normally has many useful tools on this subject.
3. Remember, there is no such thing as zero risk. You may have all your money in a bank account with little risk of default, but the risk of inflation eating up your spending power can be very damaging.

Week Eleven: The Importance of Having an Adviser

My grandfather used to say that most successful people have these three professionals in their lives: a good accountant, a good lawyer, and a good financial planner. In Proverbs 15:22, Solomon is very clear about the importance of advisers: "Plans fail for lack of counsel, but with many advisers they succeed." Now, this is not just when it comes to finances, but in all aspects of our lives. To learn the Word of God, we must have a good pastor to teach us. In school we need good professors to teach us our academics. At home we need good parents to raise, love, and prepare us for the world. I could go on and on about the different types of advisers in our lives and their importance.

This is very true when it comes to our finances. I rely on a good accountant to help me properly file my taxes. Even though I understand a great deal in this subject, I also know that a professional is better suited to perform this job. As for legal advice, I would strongly recommend that you seek the guidance of a competent lawyer, especially when you are creating your estate plan. You would be amazed at the mistakes I have seen and the unneeded expenses because people did not employ an attorney to help them draft the estate-planning documents. Finally, I believe it is very important to work with a trusted financial adviser or planner. They can assist you in creating a plan that will help you take the guesswork out of planning for things such as retirement and education.

Remember, Solomon didn't say plans fail because of lack of effort, but because we do not seek the guidance of advisers.

Questions and Study

1. To find a good adviser, first start by asking the people you trust the most. See who they work with and what their experience has been. You could also go to the Certified Financial Planner's website and search for an adviser in your area.
2. I would also recommend finding an adviser who also shares your values. This does not mean that they are going to be any better, but you will be working with these people on very personal issues, and sometimes it is nice to work with someone you can relate to.

Week Twelve: Should We Cosign on a Loan?

The economy of the United States is built on the consumer. People normally utilize credit to buy things, and unfortunately, sometimes they are not good stewards of their spending. This results in a low credit score, which makes it hard to obtain a loan for things such as a car or house. A way around that would be to cosign with someone who has good credit. God says to be very careful when cosigning. In Proverbs 17:18 God warns us by saying, "A man lacking in judgment strikes hands in pledge and puts up security for his neighbor." He also says in Proverbs 22:26, "Do not be a man who strikes hands in pledge or puts up security for debts."

We can clearly see that God is not only warning us about cosigning, but also warning us to avoid it altogether. When you sign a note with someone else, you must understand that it is *you* who has borrowed the money. The reason people need cosigners is because they are unable to obtain the loan on their own.

I remember a person who cosigned a loan with his twenty-five-year-old son for a new car. He told me that he knew he shouldn't have done it because his son was always having financial troubles, but he loved him and would do anything for him. Not more than two months later his son lost his job and was unable to pay on the loan. Now the father who was barely paying his own bills had to pay the five-hundred-dollar-a-month car payment. His new financial troubles caused by his son hurt his marriage and the relationship with his younger children. My goal with that story is not to scare you into not helping your children when they are trying to get started in life, but to use extreme caution when cosigning with anyone, even if he or she is a member of your family.

Questions and Study

1. If someone asks you cosign, ask yourself these questions:
   a. Are you willing to risk your credit and many other things in your life for this person? *Can you repay the loan if he or she defaults?
   b. Do you understand that a collection agency will go after all of your assets until the loan is repaid?
2. Read Proverbs 6:1–5.

Week Thirteen: The Patience to Build

My father told me a long time ago about the four principles to being financially independent. They are the willingness to learn, the discipline to save, the courage to invest, and the patience to build. I would like to talk about the last principle. We have all heard the saying "Rome wasn't built in a day." Normally that is said to us when we are being impatient about accomplishing some task. When it comes to investing and financial planning, patience is a must. Richard Stoker, a good friend of both Joel's and mine, said, "The road to success is always under construction." Patience is not only having perseverance or even temperament, but also being able to bear provocation, annoyance, or misfortune without complaint. A good plan will always have its setbacks, but if we remain patient, our decisions will be made with a clear head. This allows us to stay on course, even in the face of great adversity.

Psalm 37:7–9 says, "Be still before the LORD and wait patiently for him; do not fret when men succeed in their ways, when they carry out their wicked schemes. Refrain from anger and turn from wrath; do not fret—it leads only to evil. For evil men will be cut off, but those who hope in the LORD will inherit the land." I think by applying this biblical principle to our financial plans, we will be able to stick with them, and more than that, we will actually achieve our long-term goals. God has told us to be patient, and Philippians 4:6 tells us we are not to have anxiety over anything. There will be times along our financial journey when we will lose our patience and want to get rich quick, but we must remember that it takes patience to build our portfolio.

Questions and Study

1. Don't forget the other principles my father told me. If your money is sitting in a savings account earning little interest, then you should consider principle number three: the courage to invest. Also, it takes discipline to adjust your lifestyle, but you have control of your decision. Decide today to save more and spend less. Attend a financial-planning class at a local university, and be willing to learn more about investing. Each one of the principles is very important; try to integrate them into your life.
2. Look at James 1:2–4 and Romans 24:13 for more about patience.

Week Fourteen: Budgeting

Some people are very good at following a budget. They know how much they have coming in each month, and they know what they can spend. I remember a client of mine who was a teacher telling me how she never went over what she could spend on a weekly basis. She would pay all of her bills and then put an amount of cash in her wallet every week. If by the middle of week she had spent it, then she would have to go without until the next week started. By the time she was ready to retire in her mid-fifties, she had amassed a tremendous amount of money and was able to stop working.

Proverbs 27:23 says, "Be thou diligent to know the state of thy flocks, and look well to thy herds" (KJV). We should always know our financial situation. It sometimes can be a hard task but proves to be very important if we want to enjoy life without financial hardships. This is not to say that by keeping a good budget we will be free of financial problems, but it is hard to be free of financial problems without keeping a good budget.

Questions and Study

1. All well-run businesses and foundations follow a budget. It actually amazes me that the United States federal government does not follow this wisdom. Start by looking at your expenses over the past three months. Then add in anything that you pay once a year. Is it more than you bring in? How much is going to savings? How much to your church? How much is going to discretionary items such as jewelry, vacations, etc.? By doing this, you will see where everything is going, and it will be very helpful to find out what you can change. You may be pleasantly surprised or shocked. The greatest thing is that you do have the power to change your spending habits.

2. Proverbs 14:8 talks about the wisdom of having a good budget. Study this verse.

Week Fifteen: Putting It All Together

Throughout this book I have tried to take some very fundamental financial-planning topics and incorporate them into a biblical study. We have talked about insurance, investing, estate planning, and other topics that most of us will face during our lifetimes. The question is, What do I do now? Well, if any of you have ever taken a golf lesson, you know that if you try to incorporate everything the pro told you to do, you wouldn't be able to swing the club. I call this paralysis by analysis. You try to do everything at once, or you overanalyze everything until you are unable to make a decision, and nothing gets accomplished. In 1 Kings 18:21 we see the number one reason people fail financially: "Elijah went before the people and said, 'How long will you waver between two opinions? If the LORD is God, follow him; but if Baal is God, follow him.' But the people said nothing." Can you guess what it is? If you said procrastination you are correct. We have been given our free will by God, and we can use that to make a difference in our lives today.

The first step we must take is to make a decision to create a financial plan. Proverbs 21:5 says, "The plans of the diligent lead to profit as surely as haste leads to poverty." There are many resources out there, but my recommendation would be to find a competent financial planner and create a written plan. It is one thing to say what your goals are, but to write them down is a whole other story. By writing them down with a planner, he or she can create a road map from where you are now to where you want to be. Remember, to find out where you want to be, you have to know where you are. Most people I meet with say the hardest part of the financial-planning process is putting all of their information together. By doing this, you are able to create a comprehensive plan that looks at all aspects of your financial affairs. Don't just focus on one part; make sure all areas are covered. Jesus was clear about the importance of a comprehensive plan in Luke 14:28–30: "Suppose one of you wants to build a tower. Will he not first sit down and estimate the cost to see if he has enough money to complete it? For if he lays the foundation and is not able to finish it, everyone who sees it will ridicule him, saying, 'This fellow began to build and was not able to finish.'"

Questions and Study

1. Make a decision today to plan for your future.
2. Put together all of your financial documents. Here are some examples of what you will need: life insurance policies (group and personal), disability insurance policies, homeowner's and auto policies, 401(k) and investment statements, estate-planning documents (i.e., wills, power of attorney).
3. Write down your budget.
4. Take a deep breath, pray, and know that God loves you. You too can be financially independent!

About the Certified Financial Planner™

Ned is executive vice president of Kissinger Financial Services, Inc., in Hunt Valley, Maryland, a division of Sanders Morris Harris Group, Inc., of Houston, Texas. The firm ranked in *Fortune* magazine's list of America's fastest-growing companies for two consecutive years (2004–2005). After graduating from Gettysburg College, Ned worked for Merrill Lynch at their district headquarters located in downtown Washington, D.C. In July 2001, Ned and his wife, Margo, moved to Fallston, Maryland, when he took his current position at Kissinger Financial Services, Inc.

Kissinger Financial Services, Inc., was started in 1982 by Ned's father, William I. Kissinger, CPA/PFS, CFP®, ChFEBC℠. Ned is a Certified Financial Planner™, Chartered Federal Employee Benefit Consultant, and Certified Financial Educator. One of his specialties is helping individuals make wise decisions in their financial planning and investing. He conducts retirement classes at many local universities and colleges in the Baltimore area as well as being a benefits and financial-planning instructor for the preretirement courses sponsored by the Baltimore Federal Executive Board and many other federal government agencies.

Ned and his family are very active in their church, Finished Work Ministries. He serves on the board of trustees, frequently preaches, and does local mission work. He also helped in establishing and building this new church in 2004. Ned is the author of *The Battlefield of Retirement: Stories and Strategies from the Front Lines*.

In today's complex world, Ned realizes the importance of preparing and educating people to help them achieve their financial goals.

Contact: ned_k@kissingernet.com

Microbusiness General Outline
(especially for teenagers/young adults)

I. God, you, and prosperity

    A. God's purpose in creation (blessing/curse)

    B. God's purpose in redemption and the ministry of Jesus

    C. God's promises to you

    D. Conditions for God's prosperity

        1. Faith

        2. Work

        3. Integrity

    E. Terms to be defined

        1. Blessing

        2. Curse

        3. Work

        4. Integrity

        5. Redemption

II. Defining the mission of your business

    A. Your product or service

        1. Describe your product in detail. How well do you know your product?

        2. How it is different from your competition's products or services?

    B. Your market—future customers

        1. Describe in detail the people who will buy your products or services. How well do you know their routines, needs, preferences, and budgets?

2. Where is your market?

C. Your distribution plan (market strategy)

1. What are your strong points and your weak points? How do you plan to make a profit with your product in the market?

2. What are the strengths and weaknesses of your competition? How do they make a profit or fail to make a profit in the market?

3. What tools, merchandise, or help do you need to prosper in this business? Do you need to make changes?

D. Your business mission statement: Write it out using the information you have defined in the first three points.

E. Terms to define

1. Market research

2. Market analysis

3. Market trends

4. Market

5. Products and services

6. Customer

III. Money management

A. What does it mean to make a profit?

1. Define "profit."

2. Pricing—goal: Satisfy customers so they will return; satisfy the company so it makes a healthy profit.

3. The importance of profit margins as opposed to profit volume

4. How to receive payment

5. How to keep inventory

6. Keeping down costs

B. *Managing money*

    1. Paying accounts on time and understanding billing, suppliers, credit, and interest

    2. Meeting the needs of your business and your own personal needs

    3. Wisely reinvesting in your business to make it grow

    4. Savings

C. *Terms to define*

    1. Profit

    2. Profit margin

    3. Billing

    4. Credit and interest

IV. Getting and keeping customers

A. *What makes people choose one business over another?*

B. *Promotions*

C. *Customer relations (business—not products but people)*

D. *Terms to define*

    1. Bonuses

    2. Premiums

    3. Discounts

    4. Free trials

    5. Giveaways

    6. Contests

    7. Demonstrations

    8. Sales

V. Giving your business over to God

    A. Make a commitment to be a Christian business and to prayer.

    B. Become a giver.

        1. Tithing

        2. Firstfruits

        3. Offerings

        4. Acts of charity

More Words Worth Embroidering

Never argue with a fool. People might not know the difference. —Anonymous

The world is moving so fast these days that the man who says it can't be done is generally interrupted by someone doing it. —Elbert Hubbard

Our life is a gift from God. What we do with that life is our gift to God. —Anonymous

A man wrapped up in himself makes a very small parcel. —Anonymous

To fly, we have to have resistance. —Maya Lin

A man is as big as the things that annoy him. —Anonymous

Those who try to do something and fail are infinitely better than those who try nothing and succeed. *(adapted)* —*D. Martyn Lloyd-Jones*

Nobody got anywhere in the world by simply being content. —Louis L'Amour

The dictionary is the only place where "success" comes before "work." Hard work is the price we must pay for success. You can most accomplish anything if you're willing to pay the price. —Vince Lombardi

Aim for success, not perfection. Never give up your right to be wrong, because then you will lose the ability to learn new things and move forward with your life. —David M. Burns

When you have to make a choice and don't make it, that is in itself a choice. —William James

If God shuts one door, he opens another. —Irish proverb

At night turn all your worries over to God. He's going to be up all night anyway. —Anonymous

The army of Israel looked at Goliath through the eyes of man and said he's too big to beat. David looked at him through the eyes of God and said he's too big to miss. —Walley Carter

The devil can wall you round, but he cannot roof you in. —Hudson Taylor

We cannot direct the wind but we can adjust the sail. —Anonymous

A problem is a chance for you to do your best. —Duke Ellington

The secret sin on earth is an open scandal in Heaven. —Chuck Swindoll

It takes a lot of things to prove you are smart, but only one thing to prove you are ignorant. —Don Herold

The creation of a thousand forests is in one acorn. —Ralph Waldo Emerson

A man rarely succeeds at anything unless he has fun doing it. —Anonymous

If you were put on trial for being a Christian, would there be enough evidence to convict you? —Anonymous

The only thing that the average Christian wants out of Christ is an escape ticket from Hell. —Anonymous

Make sure that when you leave a person, he or she is closer to Jesus than when you first met him. —Anonymous

There is no pit so deep that God is not deeper still. —Corrie ten Boom

Most Christians read just enough of the Bible to make themselves miserable. —Earl H. Merritt

No man really becomes a fool until he stops asking questions. —Charles P. Steinmetz

Sow an act, and you reap a habit,
Sow a habit, and you reap a character.
Sow a character, and you reap a destiny. —Charles Reade

Try not to become a person of success but rather try to become a person of value. —Albert Einstein

I cannot give you the formula for success, but I can give you the formula for failure, which is: try to please everybody. —Herbert B. Swope

An intelligent person learns from his or her own mistakes, but a wise person learns from someone else's mistakes. —Anonymous

Worries are the advanced interest we pay on troubles that may never come. —Anonymous

Don't be afraid to give your best to what are seemingly small jobs. Every time you conquer one it makes you that much stronger. If you do the little jobs well, the big ones will tend to take care of themselves. —Dale Carnegie

Facilitator's Guidelines

Facilitator/Leader's Guidelines Online:
information, blog, comments, and suggestions for facilitators at
emc2Leaders.com

The website has all of the updated information for emc^2 leaders. We are hoping that this website will become a living, breathing community of facilitators who share what is working and what is not working in their respective entrepreneur club experiences.

For emc^2 Facilitators: Understanding the individual expectations of each participant will help group facilitators design an atmosphere that meets everyone's needs. Some will attend because they want to grow their business. Others will attend because they are in a reinvention mode. Still others may be doing quite well, but they want to encourage others who need help. Engaging everyone will be the challenge. When forming the group, ask each participant to express his or her expectations for being part of such a group. Take notes. Common business sense, creative marketing and branding ideas/implementation, balancing home life with busy schedules, character development, personal accountability, flexibility, core values, ethics, perseverance, and a sense of humor are some of the topics that may emerge as important concepts to be considered by all.

1. View yourself as a coach. Facilitation is an art, designed to develop a group dialogue, with the facilitator stepping forward if the conversation is getting off-track or needs to go to a deeper level. Pray that the Holy Spirit guides you as you plan and as you lead the group.

2. Ask open-ended questions that foster more than "yes" or "no"

responses. The "five Ws and one H" kinds of questions (who, what, where, when, why, and how) will help enhance the clarity of issues at hand and will help draw the maximum number of people into any discussion.

3. Use icebreakers at the beginning of some meetings. Example, "Two Truths and an Exaggeration": Each person in the group shares two real events that happened in his or her life, along with one fanciful story. Here's an example: "*Number 1:* I once met the actor Robert DeNiro at a ski resort in Utah, and we rode up the ski lift together. *Number 2:* When I was nineteen years of age, I traveled on a sailboat from Los Angeles to Samoa with my father, my mother, and my older brother. *Number 3:* I ran in the Boston Marathon when I was twenty-nine years of age and was in the top one hundred finishers." The group then determines which one of the three stories is not true about the person. This is an engaging way for people to get to know each other, having a bit of fun while doing so.

4. Another icebreaker: The "Ah" and "Um" Game: Give an overview of your business for, let's say, sixty seconds without saying "ah" or "um." It's very hard for, ah, most people, um, to do. Someone with a stopwatch can make sure that everyone keeps to his or her time limit, so that the game doesn't drag into a long time waster. Small prizes (pen, candy, etc.) can be given to those who manage to give the overview of their business without "ahing" or "umming." You can also add the word "like" into the mix, especially if the entrepreneur club is made up primarily of next-generation participants.

5. Some groups have at least one person who loves to talk and who is adept at highjacking the evening by introducing topics that have nothing to do with the subject matter of the evening ("it's all about irrelevant topics"). There are also some hyperneedy individuals who are like bottomless pits, pulling everyone's focus in his or her direction ("it's all about me"). Be aware of these types of personalities, and develop a strategy for keeping the meeting moving in a productive direction, without stripping anyone of his or her dignity or self-respect in the process.

6. Respect the schedules of busy professionals by always starting the meetings on time and ending on time. If people want to hang around afterward, that's wonderful, but at least the ending time is honored for those who need to get back home.

7. Chairs in a circle may work the best until the meeting gets too large.

8. It might be good each week to have someone communicate for three to five minutes on "the wisdom lesson(s) God has taught me through my business this past month/year." The individual then gets to pick the next person to share on the same topic the following week.

9. You may get the sense that at the end of a particular meeting that you have only covered a fraction of the designated material. Feel free to continue and expand the topic with the same material the next meeting(s).

10. Because one's business is the extension of the person, you may be amazed, at times, by the emotional pain some are experiencing in their personal lives. Marriages and family relationships can get out of balance as entrepreneurs are struggling to build their businesses. And sometimes an entrepreneur has invested so much emotional and financial capital that it is hard to hear the gut-level truth about his or her failing business enterprise. Be conscious of the reality that the emc^2 meeting is not designed to do "group therapy." Embrace your limitations. You can be a good listener and may even offer some practical advice one-on-one after the main meeting is over. But deep-rooted therapeutic issues may be best handled by a trained Christian counselor. Have a short referral list of prequalified (by you) counselors who understand the unique struggles of entrepreneurs.

11. Many entrepreneurs tend to be fast-paced, quick-thinking people who do not have the time to waste attending another boring, irrelevant meeting. Some have very short attention spans. Keep current with the issues at hand, and occasionally ask your members to communicate how the meetings can improve so that your entrepreneur club is time well spent for everyone.

12. Communicate any ideas (via email) that work for your group, and we will publish them on the open forum of emc^2 website (emc2Leaders.com) so that other groups around the world can benefit from your experiences.

13. Once a month you may want to turn your emc^2 meeting into a special event with a local successful entrepreneur coming to share his or her story, along with wisdom lessons learned over the years. You can include an open forum with audience members asking questions and sharing ideas. This may turn out to be a favorite event. Emc^2 members can invite others to attend that monthly meeting to get a flavor of what your group is doing.

14. Looking for a great project for your entrepreneur club? Consider becoming the catalyst for developing your local issue of *everyday matters*®

magazine. Doing projects sometimes brings people together like nothing else can. Check out the executive summary on the website and then request the more comprehensive document to be emailed to you—YourLocalMag.com.

What a Typical Meeting Might Look Like (should run like clockwork):

Here's a meeting agenda that may work for your entrepreneur club (**90–100** minutes total for meeting):

1. Start with prayer. **3 minutes**.

2. Personal "laser-introductions" of all the participants (e.g., name, what business you are building, number of years in business, and what brought you to this meeting today). **60–90 seconds for each person** (depends on the number of people in the group).

3. Have someone communicate on "the wisdom lesson(s) God has taught me through my business this past month/year." That person then selects the person who will share next week. **3–5 minutes**.

4. Read the chapter of the book out loud together. This can be accomplished by one person or by having different people reading one paragraph until it is finished. (Be sensitive to the reality that some in attendance may deal with dyslexia or are challenged by reading in public. Make sure that there is an honorable way for people to bow out of reading in public.) **10 minutes.** (If it is a longer chapter, you may want to read only the portion of the chapter you will be covering during that meeting.)

5. Break up into small groups. Each of the groups go to separate parts of the room or another room to discuss the questions of the workbook. Each group appoints a leader whose job it is to make sure that the group keeps on schedule and then to report back to the whole group. **20–30 minutes**.

6. After the separate discussions, each group comes back to the main room, and a designated person from each group expresses a summary of the feedback from his or her group. **15 minutes** (5 minutes for each group).

7. Problems, Questions, and Solutions: A few people can share a brief overview of current challenges they are experiencing in their particular businesses. The rest of the group weighs in, sharing wisdom lessons they

have learned in similar situations. The club leader must use excellent facilitation skills to make sure that time spent on each problem and solutions is maximized. If it is a complicated personal issue, either the facilitator or a volunteer from the group can arrange to talk with the individual after the meeting or on the phone the next day. (**Depends on how much time is left.**)

8. Close with prayer. Cookies, coffee, and soda provide an opportunity for some to hang around for a while and talk if they want.

Well-Prepared Questions:

Groups function best with questions that help them observe, interpret, and apply what they find in the Bible text. The questions should be forthright enough to allow each person to take a turn as moderator, moving the group paragraph by paragraph through a chapter. The material must not assume that everyone understands Christian jargon or can easily comprehend a religious mindset.

Operating Guidelines:

1. Confine the discussion to the chapter being studied. This keeps the newcomers at equal advantage. As the weeks go by, of course, everyone's scope of knowledge enlarges, and the group is able to refer back to chapters previously studied.

2. Expect everyone to be responsible for keeping the group focused on the topic being discussed. The facilitator's job is greatly eased if others in the group help by saying, "We've gotten onto a wonderful tangent. Let's get back to the chapter."

These suggested guidelines keep a group focused:

Ground Rules for the Group: Early in the formation of an emc² group, each may want to set up its own purpose statement and a set of ground rules that everyone accepts. Below are some suggestions, which can be built on:

1. Everything discussed within the meetings is absolutely confidential. Because small businesses are the direct extension of individuals, personal matters may be brought forward to the group. If there is to be the expectation of honesty, there must be a pledge of absolute confidentiality among the members of the group. Trust,

emotional safety, and mutual respect are the foundational building blocks.

2. No one will use putdowns or personal attacks.

3. Treat others as you want to be treated.

4. God has given each person two ears and one mouth. Listen carefully before speaking.

5. The meetings are for networking, but using the meetings to recruit others into a network marketing or direct sell-type business is discouraged. I have genuine respect for these business models, but sometimes new and excited MLMers can turn off their friends and can appear pushy—as if they are viewing their friends as potential members of their downline. Chill. Keep it genuine and keep it simple. Hidden agendas can hinder honest relationships.

6. The emc^2 meetings are designed to be an emotionally safe place for people to sometimes share what others may perceive as an off-the-wall entrepreneurial idea. Judgments are not to be a part of these meetings. Treat others the way you want to be treated.

7. Meetings will start on time and will end on time. Participants are encouraged to talk afterward, if they want.

Before the first meeting:

1. Read or reread the book *If Nobody Loves You, Create the Demand*. Order a signed copy at WorkHardWorkSmart.com if you do not have it already. The workbook connects the contents of the book to the Bible, with a spiritual application, along with excellent nitty-gritty information for becoming successful in business. And my hope is that everyone attending the emc^2 meetings on a regular basis will become wildly successful on every level.

2. The book-workbook combination should give you at least six months of material for your emc^2 group, perhaps more. Some weeks are so content rich that you may discover that you will need an extra meeting or two to cover the material. Feel free to add any material you think helps increase everyone's knowledge. If it works, please communicate to us so that we can add it to our open forum exchange of ideas.

3. You also will want to take the Personality Profile (photo album) at MyGreatPersonality.com. You can also order The Freeman

Institute® workbook on the same website, which will give you an overview of how someone's personality impacts his or her entrepreneurial success.

What to do at the first meeting (especially if you are just starting an emc² group):

1. This is a very important meeting. Most of the time can be spent getting to know each other. If the group is small enough (under fifteen), perhaps every person can share the story of his or her entrepreneurial journey briefly with the rest of the group. Plus in this meeting it might be a good time to establish the expectations. Using a flip chart, write down the hopes, the fears, and the expectations of the people interested in developing an emc² group. *Here are some questions you may want to ask*:

   i. What do you hope to receive by attending these meetings?

   ii. What do you hope to give to others by attending these meetings?

   iii. What would cause you either to stop attending or to hang back, not wanting to participate.

   iv. Tell us of your past experiences with groups (the bad and the good).

   v. What are some of the elements that help groups like this remain relevant and a wise expenditure of everyone's time, and how can we utilize those elements in these meetings?

2. *Very Important*: In anticipation of the following meeting, you will want to encourage all participants to take the Personality Profile (photo album) at MyGreatPersonality.com and order The Freeman Institute® workbook on the same website, which will give them an overview of how their personality impacts their entrepreneurial success. (If someone attends that meeting without taking the Personality Profile, he or she will probably feel left out of the discussion.)

20 Reasons You're Not Wealthy

To the Facilitator: Below are 20 statements designed to provoke excellent, thoughtful discussion with the members of your emc² group and/or for personal reflection.

Break up in small groups, with each group appointing a moderator. If someone disagrees with a statement ask, Why? If someone agrees with a statement ask, Why?

Use the discussion starters to help get things going. After the allotted time, the moderator reports back to the larger group, sharing the consensus on each statement and any wisdom lessons learned. This can be the theme of the entire meeting. (If you have a smaller emc² group, all of the participants can wrestle with each question as an entire group).

Many people assume they aren't rich because they don't earn enough money. If I only earned a little more, I could save and invest better, they say. The problem with this theory is they were probably making the same argument before their last several raises. But the truth for most people, whether you become a millionaire or not, is that it has very little to do with the amount of money you make—it's the way that you treat money in your daily life. Here are 20 possible reasons why you aren't a millionaire:

1. You Care What Your Neighbors Think: If you're competing against them and their material possessions, you are wasting your hard-earned money on toys to impress them instead of building your wealth.

Discussion Starters:

i. What have you purchased that can be directly related to trying to impress someone else? What statement were you trying to make?

ii. What have you learned about yourself as you assess your material possessions?

2. You Aren't Patient: Until the era of credit cards, it was difficult to spend more than you had. That is not the case today. If you have credit card debt because you couldn't wait until you had enough money to purchase something in cash, you are making others wealthy while keeping yourself in debt.

Discussion Starters:

i. Do you know how much debt you owe on credit cards at the moment and at what interest percentage?

ii. In what ways can credit cards be used for the good? And what ways can they be used for the bad?

3. You Have Bad Habits: Whether it is smoking, drinking, gambling or some other bad habit, the habit is using up a lot of money that could go toward building wealth. Most people don't realize that the cost of their bad habits extends far beyond the immediate cost. Take smoking, for example: It costs a lot more than the pack of cigarettes purchased. It also negatively affects your wealth in the form of higher insurance rates and decreased value of your home.

Discussion Starters:

i. What habit(s) (good or bad) do you have?

ii. How much money does your habit(s) drain from your budget in a year?

4. You Have No Goals: It is difficult to build wealth if you haven't taken the time to know what you want. If you have not set wealth goals, you are not likely to attain them. You need to do more than state, "I want to be a millionaire." You need to take the time to set saving and investing goals on a yearly basis and come up with a plan for how to achieve those goals.

Discussion Starters:

i. What are your *written* goals? For the next month? For the next six months? A year from now? Five years? Ten years? etc.

ii. What is the purpose of setting goals?

iii. What is it about setting goals that makes people procrastinate?

5. You Haven't Prepared: Bad things happen to anyone from time to time, and if you have not prepared for such a thing to happen to you through insurance, any wealth that you might have built can be gone in an instant.

Discussion Starters:

 i. What kinds of insurance do you have? Is it enough for every category?

 ii. In what others ways have you protected yourself from bad events?

 iii. How does trusting God fit into all of this?

6. You Try to Make a Quick Buck: For the vast majority of us, wealth does not come instantly. You may believe that people winning the lottery are a dime a dozen, but the truth is you are far more likely to get struck by lightning than win the lottery. This desire to get rich quickly likely extends into the way you invest with similar results.

Discussion Starters:

 i. If it is not too embarrassing, tell your favorite (personal) get-rich-quick story.

 ii. What lessons (if any) have you learned from that experience?

 iii. How does the "lottery mentality" impact a person's success?

7. You Rely on Others to Take Care of Your Money: You believe that others have more knowledge about money matters, and you rely exclusively on their judgment when deciding where you should invest your money. Unfortunately, most people want to make money themselves, and this is their primary objective when they tell you how to invest your money. Listen to other people's advice to get new ideas, but in the end you should know enough to make your own investing decisions.

Discussion Starters:

 i. Even if you have a financial planner, how closely do you watch your investments?

ii. What percentage of your investment dollars do you have in low risk, medium risk and high risk investments?

iii. How much money do you have in savings—available for you to use at a moment's notice?

8. **You Invest in Things You Don't Understand**: You hear that Bob has made a lot of money doing it, and you want to get in on the gravy train. If Bob really did make money, he did so because he understood how the investment worked. Throwing your money at an investment without fully understanding how it works will keep you from being wealthy.

Discussion Starters:

i. Tell a story about investing in something that you did not understand.

ii. What lessons (if any) have you learned from your experiences?

9. **You're Financially Afraid**: You are so scared of risk you keep all your money in a savings account but when inflation is accounted for, you actually are losing money. Yet despite knowing this, you refuse to move it to a place where higher rates of return are possible because you are afraid you will lose money.

Discussion Starters:

i. Does this apply to you? How?

ii. How have bailouts of the banking/financial community and infamous Ponzi-type schemes (e.g. Madoff) affected your attitude about investing your money?

10. **You Ignore Your Finances**: You take the attitude that if you make enough, the finances will take care of themselves. If you currently have debt, it will somehow resolve itself in the future. Unfortunately, it takes planning to become wealthy. It doesn't magically happen to the vast majority of people.

Discussion Starters:

i. If it is not too embarrassing, tell a personal story about ignoring finances.

ii. What (if anything) have you learned as a result?

11. You care what your car looks like: A car is a means of transportation to get from one place to another, but many people don't view it that way. Instead, they consider it a reflection of themselves and spend money every two years or so to impress others instead of driving the car for its entire useful life and investing the money saved.

Discussion Starters:

i. How much does a brand new car lose in value the moment it is purchased and driven off the lot?

ii. Are you hooked into having the latest and greatest vehicle? Why or why not?

iii. What have you learned over the years about your automobile and how you relate to it?

12. You feel entitlement: If you believe you deserve to live a certain lifestyle, have certain things, and spend a certain amount before you have earned enough to live that way, you will have to borrow money. That large chunk of debt will keep you from building wealth.

Discussion Starters:

i. What does the word *entitlement* mean to you and how have you felt entitled or deserving in your life?

ii. How has the feeling of *entitlement* caused you to spend money or go into debt?

13. You lack diversification: There is a reason one of the oldest pieces of financial advice is to not keep all your eggs in one basket. Having a diversified investment portfolio makes it much less likely that wealth will suddenly disappear.

Discussion Starter:

i. Draw a diagram of the diversification of your investment portfolio, indicating high, medium, and low risk investments. Are you pleased with what you see? Why or why not?

14. You started too late: The magic of compound interest works best over long periods of time. If you always say there will be time to save and invest in a couple more years, you will suddenly find retirement is just around the corner and there is still nothing in your retirement account.

Discussion Starters:

i. Comment on your age and your retirement plans.

ii. Are you happy with your progress from a financial perspective? If not, why? If so, why?

15. You don't do what you enjoy: While your job does not necessarily need to be your dream job, you need to enjoy it. If you choose a job you do not like just for the money, you will likely spend all that extra cash trying to relieve the stress of doing work you hate.

Discussion Starters:

i. On a scale of 1-10 (10 being ecstatic) how much do you enjoy what you do?

ii. If your enjoyment is low, what would you rather be doing and how realistic is it for you to change your direction?

iii. How many steps and how long would it take for you to move from where you are to a job that you would enjoy doing?

16. You don't like to learn: You may have assumed that once you graduated from college, there was no need to study or learn. That attitude might be enough to get you your first job or keep you employed, but it will never make you rich. A willingness to learn to improve your career and finances are essential if you want to eventually become wealthy.

Discussion Starters:

i. How much time (give a number) do you spend a week on personal development? Are you comfortable with that number?

ii. Where can you engage the learning process and in what ways?

17. You buy things you don't use: Take a look around your house, in the closets, basement, attic, and garage and see if there are a lot of things you haven't used in the past year. If there are, chances are all those things you purchased were wasted money that could have been used to increase your net worth.

Discussion Starters:

i. Take and inventory on the stuff you haven't used in the past 12 months. What are you going to do about it?

ii. What is the difference between a *need* and a *want*? Which one are you drawn to most of the time? Why?

18. You don't understand value: You buy things for any number of reasons besides the value the purchase brings to you. This is not limited to those who feel the need to buy the most expensive items, but can also apply to those who always purchase the cheapest goods. Rarely are either the best value, and it is only when you learn to purchase good value that you have money left over to invest for your future.

Discussion Starters:

i. What does it mean to understand the concept of *value*?

ii. Are you a person who knows how to shop for things (business, personal, recreational, etc.)? What have you learned?

19. Your house is too big: When you buy a house that is bigger than you can afford or need, you end up spending extra money on debt payments, taxes, upkeep and things to fill it. Some people will try to argue that the increased value of the house makes it a good investment, but the truth is that unless you are willing to downgrade your living standards (most people are not) it will never be a liquid asset or money that you can ever use and enjoy.

Discussion Starter:

i. How does the size of your living quarters fit in with your needs (not wants) and your current financial portfolio?

20. You fail to take advantage of opportunities: There has probably been more than one occasion where you heard about someone who has made it big and thought to yourself, "I could have thought of that." There are plenty of opportunities if you have the will and determination to keep your eyes open.

Discussion Starters:

i. What opportunities have you taken advantage of and what opportunities have you missed?

ii. How do you know when a viable opportunity appears and is something to be seized?

iii. How important is having a life mission statement so that you can determine when the *good* opportunity is the enemy of the *best*? Do you have a written life mission statement? If not, when?

By Jeffrey Strain, special to TheStreet.com. Used by permission. (Content was originally two lists; both titled: *10 Reasons You're Not Rich*). Discussion starters added by Joel Freeman.

In reality, it is probably not just one of the above bad habits that has kept you from becoming a millionaire, but a combination of a few of them. Take a hard look at the list, and do some reflecting. If you want to be a millionaire, it's well within your power, but you'll have to face the issues that are currently keeping you from creating that wealth before you will have a chance to call yourself one.

ABOUT THE AUTHOR

Joel A. Freeman, PhD—Accomplished author. Internationally sought-after conference speaker and workshop facilitator. Professional counselor. Success/business coach to executives. Behavioral analyst. Organizational culture-change specialist. Corporate trainer. Motivational consultant and mentor to pro athletes. Multiculturally astute. Photographer. Award-winning filmmaker. Experiencing an on-going love/hate relationship with technology. Passionate about dynamic, fun-filled excellence. Off-key singer and very bad dancer. A life motivated by curiosity. No bull. No hype.

Born in Maine (1954) and raised in a small town in Alberta, Canada, Joel A. Freeman brings a rich reservoir of personal experience blended with contagious enthusiasm, clarity, and down-to-earth humor to empower people from diverse walks of life with improved communication skills and maximized productivity.

The Freeman Institute®, of which Dr. Freeman is CEO/president, is a Maryland-based company with six main arenas of expertise:

I. Seminars, workshops, conferences, presentations, corporate training, staff development

II. Long-term organizational culture change

III. Executive coaching, specializing in critical incident debriefings (CID)

IV. Cultural awareness/competency and black history

V. Entrepreneurship/business intelligence and creativity

VI. Open registration seminar events (leadership, entrepreneurship, etc.)

With a PhD in counseling, Dr. Freeman served as mentor/chaplain for the NBA's Washington Wizards (formerly the Bullets) for nineteen years ('79–'98). Freeman facilitates many seminar programs, including the popular:

"Dealing with People Who Drive You Crazy!"®

"A White Man's Journey into Black History"®

"All Stressed Out and No One to Choke"

"Diversity: The Value of Mutual Respect"

"When Strangling Someone Isn't an Option."

"IGNITE (or re-ignite) Your Entrepreneurial Passion!"

Listed in Marquis *Who's Who in the World*, Freeman facilitates seminars with leaders in the federal judiciary, music and entertainment industries, corporations, government agencies, and heads of state of other nations.

The Freeman Institute® is the owner of an impressive black history collection (oldest piece dated 1553). Freeman has received rave reviews for his black history and diversity presentations. With well over 500,000 copies in print, Freeman's six books and three DVDs have received rave reviews worldwide, endorsed by Steve Forbes, Ken Blanchard, Tony Evans, Pat Williams, Bill Cosby, Teri Woods, Julius (Dr. J) Erving, Joe Frazier, Ben Carson, and Billy Graham, and are published in twenty-eight foreign translations:

1. *Return to Glory: The Powerful Stirring of the Black Man* (book and film)

2. *Kingdom Zoology: Dealing with the Wolves, Serpents and Swine in Your Life*

3. *Living with Your Conscience without Going Crazy*

4. *When Life Isn't Fair: Making Sense Out of Suffering*

5. *A White Man's Journey into Black History®* —123-minute DVD

6. *Professional Bloodsuckers: Dealing with the People Who Drain You of Your Time, Energy and Patience*—26-minute video

7. *If Nobody Loves You, Create the Demand: A Powerful Jolt of Entrepreneurial Energy and Wisdom*

Joel Freeman resides in Maryland with his wife, Shirley, and their four children, David, Jacob, Jesse, and Shari.

For information, write: The Freeman Institute®, P.O. Box 305, Gambrills, Maryland 21054

Please visit the websites below for other great titles and ideas:
FreemanInstitute.com
WorkHardWorkSmart.com
emc2clubs.com
emc2Leaders.com
eConnectRadio.com
OutreachMag.com

For information regarding author interviews or speaking at your next event, contact:
410-729-4011 or info@FreemanInstitute.com.

emc^2

Entrepreneur Ministry Club Connection

~ an entrepreneur club for the business owners in your congregation ~

If Nobody Loves You, Create the Demand
— Resources —

available at bookstores everywhere

- Book
- 4-CD Audio Book
- Workbook (especially designed for faith-based organizations)
- emc^2 membership coin

Leader's Guide:

Emc2Leaders.com

For more emc^2 information:

emc2clubs.com

How would you like to develop a relevant outreach tool for your church, along with an opportunity for business owners in your congregation and community to advertise their respective goods and services?

Everyday Matters® Magazine
everyday issues for everyday people

Dr. Ben Carson is the subject of the lead/cover article, with an insightful interview. *Everyday Matters® Magazine* is a free, educational, outreach project from the church for your community at large with an emphasis on making families stronger. Nothing in the magazine is time-sensitive, which makes it an outreach tool that can last for two to three years, until the next edition is developed. The articles in the magazine are designed to address reader-friendly "felt-need" issues, such as:

- *Men and Their Emotions*
- *How to Fight the New Bullies (teens using the anonymity of the Internet to harm others)*
- *Taking Care of Aging Parents*
- *Raising Kids without Raising Your Voice*

This unique 32-page magazine can energize the outreach of your church— paid for by ad sales and distributed FREE at grocery stores, doctor's offices, businesses, and neighborhoods within a 5–7 mile radius of your church.

We have done all of the "heavy lifting" so that the work on your end is not nearly as much if you were starting a professional-looking magazine like this from scratch, without draining one penny from your church budget. Check out the website below and ask us how the members of your emc² group and your entire congregation can win. If your church qualifies, we will email you a document with all of the fine print, including an agreement.

YourLocalMag.com